Kissitudes

of Life

The Best of Arthur Weil

Volume II

Kissitudes
of Life

The Best of Arthur Weil

Volume II

Copyright 2017 by Arthur Weil.

Printed in the USA by United Graphics Incorporated

Other titles by Arthur Weil:

A Mental Meal: Best of Arthur Weil Volume I
Illusion Diffusion
Word Shots
Eat My Words
Dare-Devilish and Divine
Have Fun While You Can
Words to Fly With
Life, Love and Gems That Shine
Exploding Mind (or 'Not Over the Hill Yet')
Poetry is for Sissies
Reflections of the Moment
The Fluid Word
Slice of Life
Theater of Thoughts
Love Always
Liquid Words
Not Shakespeare, Just Me
Wacky and Wonderful, Wireless Words
Word Missiles, Here and Now

To request other books, please visit me at my website:

www.poetrypearls.com

or download some of my books from Smashwords.com

I would like to thank
Alison Clarke Bodden,
my invaluable long-time assistant, editor, designer and book producer.
Without her help, this *"Best Of"* poetry book would not have come to fruition.
For her I am greatly thankful.
AW

Table of Contents

Nothing Stands Still   6

preamble: *a short biography*   7
Early Memories (part 1)
My Family (part 1)
Early Memoires (part 2)
My Family (part 2)
I Am That Child
The Winds of Change
1938: To America
View To The Outside
Survive
Flashes of Childhood
1938: To Chicago
The Past
I Am Everyman

chapter one: *life*   27
Doors
En Eventful Day
I Will Razz, Rip-Roaring
Life
Human Beings
The Day
Impossible
Wish and Stare
Tainted Morning
A Spit In The Ocean
Just For Me
I Can See Them All

chapter two: *holocaust/WWII*   37
Lieselotte
One Holocaust is too many!
It Never Happened
Uprooted
Memories of my childhood
Almost Holocaust
Holocaust Victim
Auschwitz

chapter three: *natural forces*   47
Evaporate
Liquid Monster
As The Earth Spins
Rain
Snow Blanket
Illusion - Scenic Mountain Top
The Horizon

chapter four: *health and aging*   57
Is Old Old?
Old Folks
Every Day
Reminisce; Making the Most of Life
Morning Awakening
Dreamer
Reborn
You Are The Driver
One Silver Hair

chapter five: *writing*   67
Great Surprise
Poets Paint Life's Dreams
Words
Pen
WHY?
These New Poets
Simple
Inspiration
I Am The Poet

chapter six: *ethereal*   77
Dreamers
Flying Feather
Share a Dream
Blithe Spirit
Dream
To Relax
Act at Last
Invisible Waves
Slew a Dragon
Soar Like An Eagle

chapter seven: *people*   87
Away, the Troubles of the Day
Just Happiness
Rich Recall
Trust
The Egotist
The Transformation
Shopping Cart
Homeless
The Modern Hermit

chapter eight: *civilizations in turmoil* 97

Nighttime
Time for Retribution
Civilization
Memorabilia for Mars
Omnipotent Power
There Was a Time
Just For Me
The Tyrant Rules
The Prisoner!
Ever Obedient

chapter nine: *the future of humanity* 107

Humanity
Rambling for a better, safer world
Nourish the World
Accept My Fate
Life
Encounters
Hope for Mankind
Who We Were, Who We Will Become
From Six Feet Under

chapter ten: *love and other bugs* 117

The Chase
Just Met
Give Me a Hug
We Hugged
Song of Love
Missing Parts
Connections In A Desperate World
I Sing A Song of Love
My Valentine
Shotgun Wedding
Love's Passion
Too Late To Cry

chapter eleven: *nonsense* 127

Putting Out
Manners
Learned It Long Ago
Neither A Borrower nor a Lender Be
Sternness
Obsessively Busy
Sometimes
Boring Speaker
Lapping Up Your Tale
Possessed
The Deal
My Special Day
Fake Facade

chapter twelve: *ponderings* 137

Some Silly Ifs
Unshackled
Nature
Drowning in Creativity
Love the Greatest

Thank you for picking up this book.

Congratulations!

You know, in today's "soundbite" world, people barely read an average of five books a year. In the following pages you will hopefully find some gems, thoughts and rhymes to stimulate as I pour out love and effection as well as some tragedy that sometimes befalls all of us.

I hope a few pages of my book will enrich and expand your horizons.

Nothing Stands Still

Nothing stands still
Always in motion, emotion
Those creative grey cells connect and jump
Even sedentary, the active mind pushes
Schemes, often frightful, concerned

Sharp, quick, my gray cells stimulate, active
I walk, I see, I observe, study or simply meditate
Yet my thoughts flow like the rapid river
Of turbulent waterfalls, or just a constant
Ripple, as heavenly ideas percolate, brew

So here I lie, or stand
Nothing stays still
I dare not wish it otherwise
Here, the colorful bouquet of flowers
Mine to observe with the earth around me

Introduction: A Short Biography

Early Memories (part 1)

When I was between four and seven, my mother, Mutti, used to take me on holiday from our home in Hanover, Germany by train to her father's family apartment in Königsberg, East Prussia, on the Baltic Sea (now Kaliningrad). Later, in 1944, towards the end of WWII,

1929 Art and Mother
East Prussia

the Russians occupied Königsberg the way Crimea is occupied today, and most Germans were removed. It was a long arduous trip and we had to transfer trains. Of course at that time the train was sealed as it passed through Poland, then into Prussia which was part of Germany, but physically separated.

East Prussia 1933
Arthur 2nd from R on top

I am second from right, on boy's shoulders

My favorite parts of these trips were visits to the Kranz seaside resort, and the beaches on the North Sea. It took an hour to get to them, and I loved sinking my feet into the sand, excited by the North Sea ocean waves. I loved the dunes, the waves, and the wild strawberries growing in the nearby forest inland. They were tiny and sweet. By 1932, due to the world-wide depression, unfortunately my grandfather lost his business and moved from that home to an elegant apartment in Königsberg, which was quite customary at that time.

For several summers in the mid 1930's I also went to a small private farm with a group of five other boys. Mutti would take me to the train station to meet them. Although aromatically it was not pleasant, we had a lot of fun. For a city kid, it was quite an experience! We took many day trips, for example on a Weser River boat ride. Often my best friend Justus accompanied me on these camps.

My Family (part 1)

I remember my mother's brother, Uncle Max, a brilliant, successful clothing designer, and his slim, elegant sister Elli, who married a non-Jewish insurance executive. Theirs was a loving ten-year marriage, but with no children. At first, my grandfather disowned him, since he was not Jewish, but over the years he eventually accepted his son-in-law. When Elli's husband was about to lose his job in 1939 (because he was married to a Jew), they divorced on a temporary basis, hoping to be later reunited after Hitler's demise. She and Uncle Max then fled to Holland or Belgium, only to be caught by the SS. We never heard from them again.

Charlotte & Siegfriend 1924

My mother, educated in East Prussia, near the Polish border, was a wonderful cook and always cooked delicious East Prussian food; Falscher Hasenbraten ("false hare roast"), various tasty chicken dishes, rice with butter and cinnamon and sugar cookies. We often had fresh fruit; apples, Erdbeeren, plums, cherries, pears, a little pineapple or tropical fruits, and also peas, carrots, eggs, and sometimes smoked fish. I remember her matzo balls, which my daughter Judy has been trying to replicate for 35 years! Mutti was an excellent baker too, and made Strudel, cherry and peach flans, but her specialty was lemon meringue which was out of this world! She also made an unbelievable recipe for eggnog.

By 1945, I was the only child of my generation on my mother's side. Out of six siblings on her side of the family, two died early on, and I was the only grandchild. I was actually named after one of her brothers, who had died shortly after WWI.

Early Memories (part 2)

Sometimes, as a child, I went to the local Hanover Zoo. I had an affinity for the orangutan and chimpanzees which are still featured there today, and also the many snakes in their terrariums. I looked forward to watching the city motorcycle races in Hanover every year. They lined the streets with miles and miles of hay bales. I would regularly walk to the Planetarium, not far from home, with school. They had a Zeiss Eagle lens apparatus which showed a replica of the solar system.

Although I could afford the bus fare through town, I would run on my skinny little legs ahead of the bus to see if I could beat it, and save some pfennigs at the same time. These were all good memories. I was relatively spoiled and sheltered as an only child. Also I was a dreamer and had a knack of rhyming, and mentally composed stories, in German of course. Even now it is very easy for me to rhyme – now in English. I have thousands of poems in my computer here in Piedmont, California, and have published twenty-two poetry books. It has been my passion and hobby since I retired.

While other kids around me joined the Hitler Youth, at the age of nine my mother signed me up with the *Bund Deutsch-Jüdischer Jugend* (German-Jewish Youth Group). I was always into nature: I caught garden snakes, *Maikäfer* (Maybugs) in a cigar box, watched them build the *Maschsee*, an artificial lake in our local park in Hanover with a beach, swim facilities and some pleasure boats. I used to walk above the River Leine (a local creek). For a penny or two I bought *Lakritze* (licorice), went to a local store that transformed into a "Flea Movie House" to watch Saturday afternoon silent movies of Tom Mix and others, and of course the recent newsreel, all for 10 pfennig. A lot of these activities I did alone, as it was still very safe on the streets back then.

> *You have your own plans*
> *Fate has its own*
> *And you know who is going to win...*

My Family (part 2)

On the religious holidays of Yom Kippur and Rosh Hashanah, I accompanied my father to the big temple, bored to death. My father was not religious, but my mother tried to keep Kosher, almost impossible at the time. She had two sets of dishes, one for dairy and one for meats. Mutti was schooled in music, and was quite a talented concert pianist, and also sang. She could recite Goethe, Schiller, Heinrich Heine. Since women did not work in those days, my mother, lonely but social with her small group of women friends, played a lot of bridge. She continued playing brilliant bridge later in life in California where she lived during her second marriage. My father, in this arranged marriage, was eleven years older than my mother, was a country man, bright, well-travelled and a successful *Getreidehändler* (grain dealer) for *Gebrüder Wolfe*, a non-Jewish firm. He served all four years in WWI, earning the Iron Cross, as did his brother and brother-in-law, and was wounded on the Eastern and Western Fronts. He was in the artillery and I still have pictures of him in his uniform. His mother and brother lived in *Steinheim, Westfalia*, near *Bückeburg* and *Hamelin* (as in the Pied Piper of Hamelin), a town with a population of two thousand, and a half dozen Jewish families.

Father's mother, Ida, was a widow. She was smart, tough, with grey hair and owned a large farmhouse in *Steinheim*, two hours train ride away. When I was around nine, I would take that regional train all by myself, stopping at the many small stations along the way. I would then walk, with my suitcase in hand, to her farmhouse four or five blocks away from the station. My cousin Herbie lived there. He was the same age as me, and we buddied up and became life-long friends, until he passed away many, many years later in Skokie, IL in 2008.

I am that Child

A flashback, I see
That skinny 12 year old me
Same stirring brain
Same piercing eyes
With the ghosts of yesterday inside
Refuting gore and the lies

My ears hear the haunting cry
The mocking sound
Ridiculing, defaming, despising me -
"Jude, Jude!"
Fearful I - move on and defy
Red, black and white the Swastika
Der Sturmer, demeaning caricature
Hooked nose with damning epithets
Heil - Heil -
A giant wall-paper pattern of raised arms
The machine of clicking heels, brown shirt and SS
Wenn du nur eine Mutter hast, so danke Gott
Und sei zufrieden!

Thank God if you still have a mother,
Thank God and be satisfied.
At twelve I was shipped on an eight-day passage
Safe now in the U.S
News of the terrible Kristallnacht
The night they burned hundreds of temples
Arrested and beat thousands of innocent Jews.
Mutti and my aunts experienced this incomprehensible terror
Neighboring youth, on order, came into their house

In a few moments, all three stories
Pieces of furniture, crystal, dishes
The store, the windows
The stench of defecation
Mattresses cut,
Bed sheets torn,
No one and nothing could stop them
My uncle beaten, though innocent
Was sent to a prison cell
Grandma Omi to Auschwitz
And her son Karl to notorious Gurs, France
Died in the ashes
He proved his German loyalty in World War I

Wounded and received the German Iron Cross
But now crosses and scars
Did not matter

Of my mother's family
Only she and I survive.
Myself a small piece of life - saved
Unlike the other one and a half million children
I am alive, here, an American, a solid citizen
After a voyage of solitary struggle
Helpless against the suffering of my family
An ocean away.

I love this world.
I am that child.

The Winds of Change

From the time I was seven or eight, from our second floor apartment facing a small square, I noticed a change in my town of Hanover. In 1932 my father bought the red, yellow and black German flag and I saw him hang it out of the apartment window, while most had swastika flags. At this time it was becoming apparent that the swastika outnumbered the German flag. In the election of 1932, my father voted for the Social Democratic Party, concerned about the Hitler movement (NSDAP) which, with their marching and weekend parades in uniform, was evident everywhere. From 1932 to 1936 I heard the nightly radio broadcast news, the ranting that this Jew or that Jew stole, accused of many random, fictitious crimes. *Der Stürmer,* a Nazi newspaper, was tacked up in full sheets on large bulletin boards on *GrossenBeck Linden*. The whole newspaper was there for everyone to read. Remember, Jews only made up barely 1% of the total population!

On weekends when Father came home, occasionally he took me to the Gebrüder Wolfe's offices where he worked. I was shocked when he greeted people with a raised hand and a "Heil Hitler". We heard that oppressive greeting more and more. It was replacing the usual "hello" or "good morning", which we just didn't hear at all anymore, starting in 1933.

I overheard my mother and her friends discussing the laws discriminating against Jews. We could no longer go to the local theater or cinema, the parks and more and more often we were seeing signs on walls stating *"Keine Juden."* Anti-Semitism ran deep, even from the Christian church and especially from the ranting of Goebbels and Göring on the radio, constantly and intensely demeaning our people on a daily basis. Considering Jews made up less than 1% of the total population in Germany at the time, this was just remarkable. 1%! How could we be seen as threatening?

From 1932 onwards, by osmosis, all Jewish families froze into a fear pattern, with extra-sensory perception of their surroundings of the Nazis programs. Many were fleeing the country. The laws restricting economic activity meant that many were put out of business. In addition, the Jewish community had to pay many random fines with many restrictions directly and indirectly, out of fear and concern, and the advent of poverty. Even though the Jewish community was extremely well organized and active, there was no end to the atrocities, starting in 1932. Conditions became more and more grim and painful. If one was caught not saluting the flag during a parade, the consequences were dire and very physical, whether it involved a Jew or not. When they marched, I would hide in a doorway and keep a low profile so I did not have to salute. Inwardly I knew that what they were doing was wrong.

On the south side of Hanover, the Jewish community owned a sports complex with a small building. During 1936 at some point a group of hoodlums ransacked the building, destroying it, defecating in it, and smashing the furniture. Mind you, this was well before Kristallnacht. Of course, we could not use our playground anyway any more, since it was forbidden for us.

While I still had my own room from 1926 to 1936, I always had a small suitcase ready if I ever should have to leave suddenly, just in case. Fortunately I was never directly affected by the hatred, other than the train incident, which I will speak about later. I was young, obedient and kept my head down.

But, I always had that suitcase at the ready.

When I was ten, my father brought me to *Esslingen*, near *Stuttgart*, to stay at an orphanage. There were eighty children aged 4 - 14, and I stayed there six lonely months. It was during this time that I heard of my Uncle Arnold's death. It was the only time I ever cried as a child, since I had been taught by my father so many times that boys don't cry.

All in all, from the age of ten and a half to twelve and a half, I received no real formal education, while I was waiting to go to the US, although I did get some tutoring in English and Math. Sadly, I've lost track - there is an almost total blank in my memory for these two important years. After I left the orphanage, I lived on the closed porch of my mother's friends' apartment for a while. Luckily we never went hungry, I studied the Lexikon, the German encyclopedia, kept a small stamp collection, saw my friend Justus Schleisner from the other side of town from time to time – but most is a blank in my memory. I did hear later that on November 9, 1938, on Kristallnacht, Nazis entered the orphanage and threw all the kids out into the street. They all disappeared. This was an example of the atrocities and cruelty of that awful night.

Aside from traveling to Berlin and going to the American Consulate with Mutti in 1936, I don't recall much from the period just before I left Germany. Once I left the orphanage in Esslingen all I really remember is taking walks, playing with the other boys and other activities with the *Bund Deutch-Judischer Jugend*, and waiting for the day I would go to America.

I personally feared the Nazis (or any uniformed person) after an awful experience in 1936 when I was wrongfully arrested on the train at the age of ten and a half. An officer claimed I had stuck my tongue out at him, which I had never done. They locked me in the train compartment for several hours before freeing me, putting me on another train to meet my mother at the station. The next morning we were supposed to report to our local police station but they had no record.

I lost my childhood as many of us did.

1938: The SS New York to America

Mutti brought me by train to the port city of Hamburg, and to the SS New York, which was, ironically, a German ocean liner. Every second liner to leave port had to be a German ship, according to the Hitler government. When we had said goodbye to each other, I walked another block by myself along the pier. Always looking straight ahead, never turning back. (Indeed, I did not turn back until 1992, fifty-four years later, when my daughter and I toured Hamburg on a trip that included the concentration camp Bergen Belsen).

To the best of my recollection, the SS New York, of the Hamburg-Amerika Line, was fairly clean, world class, smaller cruise ship. Once I arrived at the boat, a chaperone took charge of about fifteen of us. We ranged in age from 6 to 15, boys and girls alike. I shared a cabin with at least one or two other boys. I don't remember how we passed the time during those nine days, but I do remember that we never misbehaved, but walked around deck a lot, enjoying the elegant service and delicious food. Fruit cocktail and orange juice were novel, new experiences for me on the ocean liner. What treats! The excitement of the voyage overcame the loss we felt.

Whilst on the liner, I spoke to many other passengers in my broken English. I realized, to my surprise, that I was more fluent than I thought. Somehow I acquired six US pennies and then three more

Indian pennies from before 1909 on that ocean voyage! They were my found treasures, and I saved them carefully. For the rest of my life I worked hard, juggled several jobs at once, always saving some money "just in case"... like in my youth, with my suitcase at the ready, "just in case".

One day, I went below deck to where the crew was. There, to my dismay, on a 30 x 40 foot wall was displayed *Der Stürmer*, with all the vicious caricatures and accusations of Jews. Since I had had a terrible experience of being questioned on the train when I was ten and a half, I quickly dashed upstairs, to the "safe deck". The next few days were frightful. I was truly shaken by the propaganda I had read and saw. Even after we landed, after passing the Statue of Liberty, I still felt stalked and scared. To my relief we finally landed in New York after a ten-day journey, on July 12, 1938.

It was a beautiful morning when, in our European short pants, we glided by the Statue of Liberty and harbored in great New York up the Hudson River. We all stood at the railings and gawked at the Statue of Liberty. I was not forewarned and she really struck me with awe. Later, I learned about Emma Lazarus, the radical poet and her inscription from *"The New Colossus"*;

"Give me your tired, your poor,
Your huddled masses yearning to breathe free,
The wretched refuse of your teeming shore.
Send these, the homeless, tempest-tossed to me,
I lift my lamp beside the golden door!"

The Statue of Liberty-Ellis Island Foundation, Inc.

I recall after landing that about five to eight of us stayed at the Washington Jefferson Hotel at 51st Street and 6th Avenue. A woman took us to the Statue of Liberty, even took us up into the arm. It was warm, we were given the freedom to walk New York's Manhattan streets, and soak in the busy atmosphere, with all its bustle and glamor. While we stayed in New York, we visited Manhattan by bus, stopped off at Radio City Music Hall for a two hour show with the Rockettes, saw a movie (I wish I could remember which!) and four of us went up the RCA building. We went up seventy stories in fifty seconds! What a view! We had never seen anything like it. The Empire State Building was fogged in but still an experience.

View To The Outside

Outside my bedroom window, early morn
Within reach, all autumn leaves, brown, curled
Have fallen
Gnarled, naked branches string downward
Hard, lifeless, gray, a bit mangled
Like some many-faceted creature
Whose tentacles in space are perilous

From strong stem to tiny bending tips
Slightly swaying, a huge monster puppet
With the brilliant sun shining on the exposed crust
Not quite dead, yet still very much alive
More like my stubborn chest cold
Struggling to recover

Almost delirious, my mind wanders
Conjures up seasons long ago when my father's emaciated form
Rang the bell, ready to enter the gates of heaven
There are still rustling leaves swept to their eternal rest
All seems dormant, waiting for a spring awakening
I peek at these memories ever so often
See visions and figures of friends far gone
So vivid, real, alive - I can almost touch

Relaxed, I stare through the square framed panes
Only a few feet from my bed
My warm comfortable room this morning
A mixture of all nature, life and memories
For seconds the tree melts into apparitions
The loved ghosts of yesteryear
New focus; the glimmer of trees beyond and above
Blue, so pure, heavenly azure, endless blue
Luckily this contemplative morn boosted thoughts
Yes, I too will recuperate
Or maybe I already facetious, but not devious
I revamp my self-imposed code of ethics

Survive

Facetious, but not devious
I revamp my self-imposed code of ethics

Accompanied by grievous guilt over nothing

Should I have them cut off all my hair?
Go bald-eagle in empathy
with stage 4 cancer victims?

Or should I build my own
holistic castle, safety net
for when life yells "nicht so schnell!"

There is a plethora of soul gold
An infusion of solid sunbeams
Catch my share of happiness vouchers!

Chuckle, overcome, survive and thrive

Enough is enough
But there is always some more

Flashes of Childhood

Aunt Ilse is on the far right, with other relatives. My cousin Walter Rinn's father is on the left. Koenigsberg, Germany, around 1930

Lengthwise, roll down the hill
Tease, push, and wrestle
Pinch each other, as little boys do
Or catch the brown, beetle-like May bugs
Antlers on their male counterparts
Trap in a spacious cigar box
Fill with green maple leaves
Abundant meal for the innocent yet pesky insect

The rustle of wind-blown leaves
Brown, yellow, piled in mini mountains
Half decomposed in the sun's rays
Dancing oblivious
Sunbeams dance of death
The cantata of chirping birds
Answering the mating call
With innocent chirps

Stunned I stand, observe, listen, and marvel
Paint the landscape with Nature's music
Step cautiously, avoid the cow dung
Cows chewing, clinking bells
While the morning crow of the rooster
Announcing the dawn
Soothes the hens, jostles
Pink pigs in their messy sty

I am just a city boy, visiting
Competitive, I jump from the roof of the barn
Into hay bales spread
Like a yellow mattress, oozing their fresh cut smell
Dry grass for the winter store
Jump again - my right hand twists
Fractured in two places
Utterly painful, my tears and anguish
Mixed with hurt pride

The surprise of sudden rain
Often ignoring shelter
Soaks to the skin
All wet and natural
This time of bliss and innocence
The laughter of those moments
Embellished in my being
How lucky to remember once more
As I reflect - 80 years later
With barely a scratch

I must have loved the world
As even today I can fly and fall
Lift my bent, older body up
Look upon the jostling maelstrom
Smile, content, excited with life
Not yet ready to define my memories
But ready for tomorrow
Tired eyes refreshed
Anxious to meet any challenge

You don't have to wait for thunder
To take cover from the storm

1938: To Chicago

My train ride to Chicago was uneventful. I took the same trip many times later in life. Five of us kids were chaperoned on the train, and three of us were dropped off in Chicago. My Aunt Ilse (my mother's younger sister) greeted me, along with the Jewish Family Services, at the station. Ilse had moved to the States four years prior. Despite an advanced education and a great talent as a designer, she still had to work in her cousin's (my grandfather's brother's family) button factory when she first arrived.

It was such a relief to see her. She gave me my very first one dollar bill. That was a lot of money, since she only earned $18.00 a week. She had by now become assistant editor of an Anti-Nazi weekly paper, with a readership of about 10,000. She was very liberal and I looked up to her greatly at that time. She was bright, athletic (she skied) but had no children. She lived in a small studio, read two books every week, and was an avid leftist reader, did not drive a car. She turned out to be one of the most influential people in my life, and I often went to her for advice. Unfortunately she died of kidney failure when she was only fifty.

Art and Ilse

Later that same day when I looked for the dollar, to my utter dismay, I couldn't find it. It must have been lost in the shuffle at the station. I never told her, of course. But I still remember the awful sinking feeling.

In Chicago's north side, we went to meet the fairly young couple who were to be my first foster family in a small two bedroom bungalow. They had a twelve year old son who shared his room with me. The family received $25 each month for fostering me. I don't remember much about them, but later I was apparently invited to their son's Bar Mitzvah and I missed the invitation, having never been told. Apparently they were disappointed that I never came... I still feel guilty about missing it!

Herb Weil, my cousin (left). I was best man at his wedding and he was best man at mine.

In front of the Indianalpolis Symphony,1946

My cousin Herbie and me on the beach in Chicago

Teaching German at Bancroft Junior High, CA

Arthur and Mutti, Charlotte

The Past

We all conjecture
Good riddance to the past
We cannot change
Wisdom and pain
The pearls and tears of yesterday
Success and failure
Teach treasures of experience
Loves won and lost deeply ingrained
Luck, coupled with disasters,
Misfortune, painful knowledge
Break then heal the purest heart
The past is ours unique, and special
Brief lamented history
Visions of parents, siblings, relatives, teachers
Reborn so vividly, elated and recoiled
Childhood friends, the escapades of youth
Our home, the place we played
Here we swam, walked, basked in nature
Our first love crush
Guilt and excitement rolled into one
We learn and re-evaluate as we mature
Impossible to erase yesterday's thoughts
Ego fed, arrogant, flagrant, and picturesque
Our brilliant mind zeros in
On her red-cheeked smiling face
The field of crocus, blanketing the landscape
A flick of celluloid alive, yet distant and far behind
The trophies of disappointment
Healed with hope, opportunities lost and gained
Vibrant gray cells in brain agitate

Stir up emotions as we relive the past
And yet the present
The face of me and you--more certain
Things come and go, in memory ingrained
So much to see, to do, to love
Now, today, tonight
Despite events in which the protagonist is powerless
The inevitable does not have to be
There is still the precious time
The joy of doing, every new venture
Dreams into reality – move, dare to start
Yours--mine. Let us celebrate now!
As now we walk side by side

With the shadow of our past

My maternal great grandmother

I Am Every Man

My mind and body
Span the continent
In every shape and color I am every man
I till the soil, excavate minerals
Clear debris, create metropolises
A combustion of man's creativity
I am every man

I announce myself, the exquisite inventor
Mixer of chemicals and potions
Create magic boxes
Vials, bottles which hold mysterious rays

Communicate within the unending universe
Fantasize, philosophize, idealize
Inventor, builder and destroyer
I am everyman

Mesmerized by my own reflection
I shape realms, safeguard with an enchanted will
And, with human folly, climb moonbeams
Only to recover on the sordid muddy soil

I am tossed like a nutshell in a pond
Rising and blown by breezes like a balloon
I am there, helpless, to observe and scan all
Until the sole of my shoe touches ground again

I, you, we
Build frames of tradition and truth
Or destroy with unseeing anger
Led by demagogues of technology and false religion

Blinded, duped, consumed with passion and hate
With a perspective, walled in by the cement of ignorance
Collective man's colossus rises
Asserts and drowns in his own abundance

1953 DePaul Grad
Art and Lillian

At the Catholic Church, DePaul University,
Chicago, graduating Magna Cum Laude,
Masters Degree

Be he heathen or bigot
The demon and demanding chemicals of the brain
And all the philosophers' warnings are cast aside
Until, too soon, the last bell rings
And I see the end of an ignorant generation
In self-destruction,
And they thirst no more
Leaving to the next to re-build and repair

While some Holy Spirit hovers to regenerate
Recoup both good and bad
You have a soul!
Who will ever know that the heart beats on
Then the heart stops and the spirit passes

I am everyman

chapter one: life

DOORS

Imagine yourself, your life
Which doors have you entered?
Ah, so many each and every day
Do you see the doors?

From space to space
In the privacy of our homes
The bathroom, basement and attic
Doors that hold secrets

You know you can enter or exit
Unsure of what you might find
Parents, youth, all bidding
Full of love, endearing

Doors of many colors
Great hopes
Openings of fear, frustration
Doors I never want to enter again

Doors once opened
Part of my youth
(If you play with pet birds
Never leave the door open)

Doors are merely extensions of
Our boxed-in lives
Doors of separation, of sound
Of smell, of life

Truly, doors are not natural
Where in the mountains and valleys
Or the expanse of open meadows
Do you see doors?

An Eventful Day

The morning wakes
Somewhat warm, incoherent
Open summer day
My choice for this Saturday
An open world

Arms held out from horizon to horizon
Almost
Moses holding the tablets
Of the Ten Commandments
With ample choice to fill

The precious hours
An air of quiet peace
Like water poured to fill a cup
So too new thought collate

So many choices
So many possibilities
It's going to be an eventful day
Struck off my life's calendar
For who knows how many
We have
Left ahead
Of us!

2014 trip to Tahoe

I Will Razz, Rip-Roaring

I will razz, rip-roaring
Simply jolly, hilarious, scoring
Like a wildebeast roaming his territory
Shout out, reveal some tale or story
Like vagabonds in years past
About a love-life made to last
Or devious calamitous scam
So undetected on the lam
So frivolous and frolic share
With wild abandonment and scare
As their army hordes near our town
All pack up and leave with grimacing frown
Or some rich dude who celebrates
His daughter's wedding at the gates
Invites all the festivities
Loose with his money all to please
And sigh and lie as lovers in the dark
Romp, rail that life is but a lark
Who cares as careless kisses fly
Consumed will love, oblivious as time goes by

Life

Ambulance sirens
 Ever drowning the silent night
  It's the cycle of our existence
   Our dreams soon dissolve, evaporate
   Yet leaves rustle, birds twitter
    A constant dizzying cycle
     We call it life
      Love and live it
       Some even die
        But many embrace
         Even in the bleak darkness
          There is heavenly unison

                And lots   and   lots of   *love*

Human Beings

How quickly life passes by
We wonder who we are
How we fit in
We are small, mobile creatures on two legs
Foraging, we use an odd mixture of concocted
shorthand
To communicate
And often to miscommunicate

King's Beach at Lake Tahoe

The Day

The day was fraught with improprieties
Strung as intermissions
Wrong clothes
Wrong words
Wrong chewing
Toothpick, fingers
Wrong flowers and gifts
The awkward etiquette
Of a civilized society
That knows how to kiss

But there's always tomorrow

Impossible

Impossible to always stay on top
Impossible to have it all
To live beyond our means
Before the diehard fall

Impossible to dream of heaven's end
Impossible to possess all
And wrap all beauteous feeling
Or nature's canvas call

Impossible to carry the world of pain
Impossible to wave the wand of peace
Shed shower of tears in sympathy again
When causes spill so deathly, most insane

Impossible to live forever
Impossible to be too clever
For mankind solid footing is quite soft
Time for peace a venture to endeavor

Impossible to live too much
Impossible to love all about
For heart and body soon disappoint
Leave shreds and agony a rout

Yet the possible in our fist
The joy of heart, of now
Look for the sparkle in our midst
Accept with humility, take a bow

Wish and Stare

One positive act is more
Powerful than 10,000 wishes

One stare into space
Can open and discover a new universe

One wrong critical pun
You're undone - no fun!

Skirmish at the border
Keep control and order

Distance from some renegade
Whose life is full of hate

Must thwart and calm his will
Ere he may anger, even kill

Go water seeds of joy
Rejoice as if new toy

Unleash the spirit holy yours within
Be true to your own friend and kin

First step to a new height
And make your future right

You are precious, you are rife
You have the gift of glorious life

There is a beginning
and there is an end
but all of my life
I have been stuck in the middle

TAINTED MORNING

Tainted morning wind and chirps break the quiet
      Now dawn, as shadows come alive
The first slow movement of today's symphony
      As tempo, beat and rhythm do accelerate
Another marvelous morn like a blooming red rose is born
      A bursting palette of color in an impressionist painting

Yet nearby the cacophony of city bustle
      Computers, forms, recipes and theories
No bloody contusion, no bowels split
      Nor the anguished cry of last night's victim
Just temporary entrenchment
      In golden search of sun's scenario

Recharged, a sensual, gradual rebirth
      Before the sunshine spreads its magical energy
Displaced with billions of penetrating, stimulating rays
      Announce the inevitable morning of grandeur and promise
Pure opportunity to be earned and enjoyed
      And blue jays still trill to their hearts' delight,

*...for he in life who does not chance
misses the music and the dance.
So stay on route to certain success
while failure skeletons leave a tragic mess.*

A spit in the ocean

Life is a pittance;
A spit in the ocean,
Precious as a fine cut diamond,
A sharp rock tossed into the ocean,
Lost among sparkling brown pebbles and myriads of sand stones
That erect creature of destiny, the Sphinx
Questions our hunger to touch the very stars glisten in the sky

We wonder at our immense appetite
As we consume flora and fauna, drink from virgin wells
Leave abundant waste, decay and chemicals
Watch pure, clear liquid become rivers of poison
And she, gigantic and beautiful, wonders if we justify existence
By forever procreating, building awesome nests
That we dig deep into the breast of the earth
Transform lush nature
Into cold and shining cities
Create myriads of beehive inventions

We are born into a world of genetics and new specimens
Thrust and pushed into fashionable particularity
Rocket to Mars, the moon and the stars
Build stadiums, fill them with sport stars
Produce creative theaters, fantastic music
Create mutants and replicas,
She sees us engulfed and drowned in our own humanity
Gasping for air in the sea of the universe
Judge ourselves and ignore

Know that this land, this great planet
Will eventually dissolve and spin no more
While a spit in the ocean is still visible

Just for Me

Sometimes in my life
All is staged
Some supernatural power
Or the observing Gods
A painful dream, a reality show
Like a cascading mountain boulder, tumbling
I partake, I survive
Just for me

My mind and spirit absorb
Tame my subconscious fears of tomorrow
Overbooked calendar, promises hard to keep
Everywhere the crash, the beat of city noises
Hustle, movement, often blindly automatic
Devour before it devours you
Cars, destinations, self-propelled
Steered dutifully and mechanically

A much blurred vision of life in all directions
The tattered, homeless, bearded man
Standing, hands out, "Can you spare some change?"
The flash of a neckline on a sexy dame
Petite, slender, wiggly, alluring
The feeling soon subsides
Huge advertising signs of unneeded food
A forest of traffic signs just to confuse

And silly, sometimes I even fantasize
This collage, this colossal drama, in juxtaposition
Is it a Greek drama and comedy combined?
Or a secret video of my daily reality?
All actors play their part
To please, cajole, collect, connive
And life's patron counteract
And earn my daily keep, just for me!

I Can See Them All

The billionaire in his twenty-bedroom mansion
The homeless skeleton crouched in the doorway
The mother carrying two bouncy tots
The cabdriver searching the streets for a fare
I can see them all

There is a storm, a cold, ill wind
A new calamitous disease spreading
A leopard escaped, running loose
Another young prostitute, beaten bloody
I can see them all

Headlines: *Wild Shooter Kills Two Year-Old*
Motorcyclist Rammed By A Car, Dead
Building Collapsed, Three Die!
Police Shoot-Out, Killer Executed
I can see them all

A dictator, a treacherous invasion
A mass refugee migration from oppression
An outbreak of cholera in tropical lands
A typhoon drowning hundreds
I can see them all

A successful heart by-pass operation
A ceremonial burial fire on the Ganges
A historical leper colony in Hawaii
A sick, weak child in the infirmary
I can see them all

A colorful balloon competition
A downhill ski race from 14,000 feet
An exciting World Series shut-out
A six-hour grueling tennis match
I can see them all

The amputee veteran
A robust, smiling, pink-cheeked cherub
The bent old toothless gal, happy as a lark
I chuckle on the inside
I can see them all

The joyous little two-year old tyke
Skinny eight year old, catching bugs
Laugh at the puppet show
And me, the innocent, happy participant
I can see us all

chapter two
Holocaust/WWII

Lieselotte

Lieselotte snapped out of her slumber
The nine year old, petite, precocious girl,
Crammed next to Mutti in this stinking cattle car.
The cramped humanity, barely room to sit or lie,
Clothes for three days, no latrine
Old, sick, coughing, indigent
Several had died already as the wagons moved on.
Ever-so often they would open up the rolling doors
Somewhere in the country.
Always the uniformed, angry guards
With their rifles, guns, dogs, harsh commands
They said, "On the way to the East; Poland!"
The sad, eerie sound of wailing, whining,
The endurance of pain - all but mesmerized

The clatter of the railroad wheels below ever moving.

Barely fourteen months ago,
Their beautiful large apartment in
Berlin Oriental carpets, book cases with leather-bound books
Lots of oil paintings adorned the walls,
An upright piano festooned with music pamphlets
Mutti was a great pianist, she even sang,
And dad, a physician, a skin specialist
Enjoyed a large, well-earned practice.

"My room," Lieselotte half dreamt and recalled,
"Had my own wardrobe, a small bookcase,
A wonderful collection of dolls
A clown picture on the wall.
And even a large dollhouse that
Mutti and Vati gave me at Chanukah.
During the holidays aunts and uncles would visit
And Ursula, my best friend (she wasn't Jewish)
Would laugh and make up droll stories.

But all that was before!"

The clatter of the railroad wheels below ever moving.

One day Mutti said, "You must go to a Jewish day school,
That's a rule and new law.
Vati can't practice at the hospital anymore
nor treat non-Jewish patients.
Not allowed to go to the Kino, the movies
To the children's' matinee on Saturday,
Or play with the other kids outside.
Our maid Justine had to be let go.

Many friends left for the United States or Palestine,
Or South America - things were getting ugly.
The raucous preaching by Hitler or Goebbels, or Goering
Drowned out any privacy.

The clatter of the railroad wheels below ever moving.

One day, on short order: "Must sell everything
and meet at the Marketplace with one suitcase each."
They say the law is the law.
"Vati always taught me to be honest and obedient
And so I reluctantly went along.
Our apartment was auctioned off in one day
And now we were headed to the Ghetto in Warsaw,
Everywhere there is poverty, hunger, stern faces.
What did we do?
We were all so innocent and overwrought."

The clatter of the railroad wheels below ever moving.

"Was it my fault that my parents were born Jewish
And taught me the ten commandments as best they could?
I must cover my ears", Lieselotte thought.
"I must close my eyes and think of good things,
Birthday parties, Friday evening dinner with the Sabbath candles,
Vacation at the Ostsee at Nordernei.
I must hope again for a festive meal."

But Lieselotte's short life, little did she
know,
Was coming to an end.
Would it be soon?
After weeks of starvation and deprivation,
Huddled in Warsaw,
The family was broken up.

*The clatter of the railroad wheels below
ever moving.*

photo credit Holocaustexplained.org

38

Later, much later, they were lined up again,
Suitcases filled with what was left.
And so now she is in the jammed cars of cattle wagons ready for,
Yes, ready for Auschwitz.
So much prospect!
So much hope!
All vanished under the voice of the Final Solution,
The extermination of all Jews.

The clatter of the railroad wheels below ever moving.

All I can say is, "Auf Wiedersehn, Lieselotte -
You and one and half million other innocent
Children; victims of a mad, prejudiced society".

   ...The clatter of the railroad wheels ceased.

*(I have students read Lieselotte out loud when
I give my Holocaust Talks to High Schools).*

One Holocaust is too many!

You may say, "Enough talk of the Holocaust!"
I say, "Never enough!"
The mere thought of the holocaust
sends shivers of fear, gruesome scenes.

Wiped out
Well educated
Peaceful
Gifted, with a code of ethics
Charity, an outstanding value system
Wiped out

Wiped out
A humanity of goodness
First tortured, starved, denigrated
An innocent, innocent people
Beyond man's imagination
Succumbed to systematic acts of cruelty
Torture
Wiped out

Wiped out
The very soul disemboweled
Spirits squashed into animalistic survival instinct
Outward pain, inward pain
Eyes perceived the beaten, starved skeletons
The ears heard the agonizing cries
Shrieks, outbursts, groans
Shrunken stomachs, walking corpses
All so innocent, but for their birth
Wiped out

Wiped out
Prejudice-ridden, rampant
The mothers' ordeal
Innocent children obliterated
By starvation, gas, bullets, beatings
Never in history has man's inhumanity
Taken such a bestial turn
To murder the innocent, weak, old and sick
And the children
Wiped out

One and a half million children
In hundreds of concentration camps
Whipped, beaten, in most painful devious thoughts
Punishment, eradication, elimination
For what purpose?
Wiped out

Wiped out
All done by hateful, indoctrinated men and women
Latched onto a sinister, stupid destructive ideology
Innocent – innocent – innocent
Where were the values?
Thousands of years of modernity?
All into the waste of ashes
The smell from chimneys still chokes my nostrils
Wiped out

IT NEVER HAPPENED

The green rolling meadow
Interspersed with foliage, trees
Casting an eerie shadow
Where starving women walked, would freeze
Anne Frank her youth decayed
The British free the living skeletons too late.
In '92 Judy and I witnessed the gruesome mounds and tombs
5,000 - 10,000 buried among new blooms
Bergen-Belsen
IT NEVER HAPPENED

Remnants on French, Austrian and Germans interred
In southern Vichy France
Uncle Karl, My father Siegfried, uncle Walter with their Iron Cross absurd
Prisoners of the SS net and Himmler's plans
Disease, starvation, a year or so – Walter died
Siegfried, my dad, with visa shipped to Martinique
And Uncle Karl in cattle cars to Auschwitz in the night
Camp Gurs
IT NEVER HAPPENED

Steinheim, Westphalia Weils; my family, rooted for hundreds of years
Orders arrest 70 year-old Ida, grandmother, loyal matron
Innocent, believer, part of 12 million tears
The ovens of Auschwitz her reward and patron
Old family farmhouse, family meadowland confiscated
Years later I received $1,000 compensation
Auschwitz
IT NEVER HAPPENED

Some did escape with soul so jarred
Branded, naked, determined to rebuild
I, 12 years old, in Chicago spared
The anguish pain of childhood now unfilled
To carry cross and torch and memory and hurt
Remnant, rebuilt, grandchildren that thrive
Serious, cognizant, unsure, alert, still very much alive
IN FREEDOM
IT NEVER HAPPENED

I mourn the gypsies, the disabled, protesters and priests
Nine million tortured, starved, died
I'm angry, pained, achinf, stalked by those uncivilized beasts
Amongst them 1.5 million children – now ghosts
Only a few torturers were tried

My daughter Judy during our visit
to Auschwitz, 2014

In France, Oct-Nov 1944. My friend
John Clark (left) and another soldier

1944 Arkansas
A Soldier on the Loose

Fort Smith,1944

Auschwitz, 2014

Uprooted

Uprooted,
ornate room
the Persian rugs
Family portrait picture on the wall
Warm harmonious kitchen
All gone

Permanent cemetery still there
People never to return

The streets of home still the same
A citizens walk about
The mask of fear erased
Strangers now occupy our homes

The sounds, the joy of gramophones
The blasting radio newscasts
"Jude, Verträter – Dieb"
Extinguished
No family Pesach,
no Friday evening
Chicken roast

Memories of my chidhood

From a state of total freedom and liberty as a young boy, with ample food, the luxury of having a maid, now we started to see the various laws of restrictions come into effect.

All culminated in the elections of 1932 and 1933 when the final nail was put into the coffin. All opposition parties were removed, there were mass arrests, edicts passed and vicious, false accusations and hate spewed all over the country.

When many places became off limits to us, we were forced to only socialize with our own religious groups. I was pulled out of public school in the fourth grade, separated from the kids on the block with whom I grew up, and restricted in every possible way. Adults were especially limited in the ability to make a livelihood and soon had to live on savings with a bleak future ahead.

I was still truly innocent, from a nine year old kids' point of view. The world was still my oyster… I studied the Lexicon, picture books of trains, cars, inventions. It was at the end of the industrial revolution. Germany had one great things going for it; it was an era of hope and opportunity. Since I did not understand politics and no one taught me, I was a happy, fearless youngster. I was totally ignorant of the deadly dark cloud beginning to choke my people.

But I learned soon enough.

Almost Holocaust

No number burned into my arm
Just all around the inside
Of my skull
Reflected in precious grey matter
Easily retrieved

So alone
No siblings
The pavement of Hanover
The walking dreamer
No bomb, no barbed wire
No aura of defeat
Escape to America
Too late after the Holocaust
Etched into my brain

Always walking
Excited with broken English
I was a wounded, mature 12-year-old
Unable to jump out of his skin
For you are what you are

I constantly asked
How could one percent of the population
Be such a hindrance?

Little time for love
For attention

Now later
I do retain some of my religion
Always trying to visualize the omnipotent God

Anxious to give love
Never learning how
With wild abandonment
I dug new roots

Holocaust Victim

Robbed of my childhood,
Bundled in smelly rags,
Humiliated to the lowest ebbs of Hell,
Stiffened with fright
Cannot distinguish day from night.
Swollen stomach, gnawing sickness,
Sunken, hollow eyes.
The heart beats,
Little hope.

Why survive?
Why stay alive?

Like a beaten, degraded animal
That has felt man's inhumanity to man,
Loved ones torn apart,
Castration, damnation.
How can other creatures
Partake in such ghastly features?
Maimed, demonstrably scarred for life

I must survive!
I must survive!

The heart beats.
There is little hope.
Boils, blood in the stool,
Bones tender and skinny,
Inflammation, degradation,
Broken shoes too tight.
Famished, underweight

Will it end?
Will we transcend?

Will the will, the soul
Survive the disaster?
As assuredly it must.

We will not die,
We will not rot,

We do believe
We have a God
We painfully shout out loud,
Rehearse and curse.

Where are you, Master of the world?
Whose bleak, black hurricane
unfurled?
Mournful, in pain
Return! Return, our gracious God,
And promise
                    Never again.

Auschwitz

The innocent mother and child
In the gas chamber lines they filed
Quashed all future love and hope
Sadistic torture, they could not cope

Millions of souls we still remember
Honor each flake of flying ember
No-one can feel the anguish and pain
The brutality by the SS they did sustain

When will it stop, too many innocents?
In these modern times it makes no sense
People, stop this insanity
And show your true humanity

*Cousin Herb Weil, who was also my best friend, at the
Holocaust memorial, Museum of the Legion of Honor,
San Francisco. His father (my Uncle Karl) and Aunt Ida died
in Auschwitz.*

chapter three: natural forces

Evaporate

The rapids gently tested
A silver stream cascades peacefully between the
Steep and narrow boulders

Now water slowly spreads
over a slivery silver glistening lake

The boat steers, placid, maneuvering easily
Heading majestically, regally downstream

to meet the wide,
inviting
open-aired lake

Only to evaporate, rekindle
With steaming grace

While the passengers are enthralled

with the exotic, awesome splendor

If you sit down and wonder long enough
It will rain

Liquid Monster

I tossed a small oval pebble
Into the becalmed, smooth ocean
Concentric circles waves growing,
The sound of waves faster, foaming, gurgling
Had the ripple effect as if to wake up
A giant monster beneath
No-one felt the ominous threat - not yet
A volcanic eruption or supposition of the moon
The becalmed ocean now a massive upheaval
As I listened to the chorus of ocean war, war
In progressive, powerful notes louder and louder
Until a crescendo crashing, thrashing
The monstrous bluish-green fluid persisted
Like boisterous boys, maniacs jumping the waves
Guided into menacing, powerful, ever-higher waves
Portent of disastrous destruction, possession drowning
Soon the volcano tempered
The moon at the far end of the hemisphere
Recoil, diminish, subdue, the furious force
Winds subside, blue cloudless sky, calm restored
Takes back the liquid monster into fabulous foamy ripples
Peacefully licking the moist, sandy brown beach
Gradually
        washing
                the corpses
                        ashore

Pacific Ocean. South of Monterey, California

BUTTERFLY

In innocence you hibernate, heal and survive
Like the larva of a butterfly
Until your great mind
Buttressed by nature's edict
Turns thought into deliberate action

And you decide, conclude
That you want to scan the world
Gather all your resources and change
From a pupa into a beautiful colorful butterfly
With an antenna that knows the direction
Looking to gather honey from flowers
And to germinate

Only to fly back home
To safety and to copulate
So please don't stick me on a pin
Display my beauty in a glass case
To please some entomologist

We are all creatures
Only
Some of us are
More
Shapely

AS THE EARTH SPINS

Spindle, top - hit it - let it turn on its axis
Rotate, my dear planet, gyrate
Gravity, motion, centrifuge
All revolves
You and I, we move with it, helpless passengers

Say, "Steady, steady, turn and turn"
It's lucky that gravity keeps us sound and upright!
No wonder the ancients thought
We were at the center of the universe
Don't even feel the earth's rotation
Yet I know there is day - night, half moon, full moon
The stars shine, while planets rotate rapidly around us

Sturdy and steady from childhood, we balance on our earth's crust
Indifferent, in innocence, unconcerned, we move
Glued by gravity we instinctively do our daily balancing act
Earth's magnet pulls our moon as the moon's mass pulls us
Lifts up the oceans, creates tides as all in our
Universe is interrelated
Yet we the unsuspecting passengers, experience, feel nothing

I am yet dizzy thinking about the spindle top topple
Never to return to that exact same position
Spinning - in motion - gravity
Always moving, but steady, not immutable
In the same cloudless, azure, endless sky
I cannot even fathom me, the unwilling passenger
Hardly recognize that this holy earth
Has its own travel plans accompanied
By nature's tumultuous seasons
While at night the reflection of moon and sun or star power
On Mars, Jupiter, all of the planets, looking down

The trillions of stars beyond, the endless skies
Impossible to imagine
Involved in my own busy dizziness

I look away from the spinning top
Know that there's an infinite world out there - all about
People, noises, demands, duty, responsibility
I am a central part of all, often oblivious
Sometimes life, like an ocean wave pulls perilously
Swallowing too much, I try to catch my breath
Regain my footing ready to combat all
A creature of intuitive existence
Always changing and yet the same

And while our massive earth
Turns in this invisible motion
Like a merry-go-round as the earth turns
With each season's mantle and blanket of colors
What delight, what euphoric feeling
We are so self-involved; who has time for the earth?
Rich seeds grow, yet we must stoop to harvest
Bury their spindly roots in the ground
And mankind imbibes in plums, apples and nectar
Celebrating the time of seasons

So lucky we can share - be there!
All senses dance, live in the now
And maybe for a short moment, forget our troubles
The snow white, rich green, dusty brown colors of the seasons
Late at night, we look up into sky
The Milky Way, the planets, the stars glistening
They are all there, and we, the witnesses, are part of them
As
        the
                earth
                        spins.

Rain

It's 12:37 A.M.
We all prayed for more rain!
Yes, our prayers were answered.
Gusts, sheets of torrential silvery rain Incessant
loud   thrashing   wet
Continuous, heavy drumming sound
Proud   most defying
Like the incessant banging of death row prisoners
The thunder of bison herds long ago
Never dying

Everywhere, pools of soggy wet
Rows of water pearls bounce on their target
Bullets against an armored tank
While receptive brown and withered autumn leaves
Plump, rain soaked from tired wet braches earthward
Deliver the cool liquid with it
Like teaspoon medicine gone wrong
Drip-drop unto the hungry earth
Distant thunder (barely audible), pronounced, eerie
Evidence of more to come.
Nature's dance, romance of centuries
Sun nurturing the openhanded land
Cycles of light rain to showers
Stirs uneasy emotions... *Wonder when will it all stop?*
As roof drains rasp, move into ever lower level places
Gutters, creeks, accept the translucent moving flow
The rivulets into roaring dirty, erratic waves
A torrent monster, unstoppable
Much more than we bargained for!

Umbrella, roof, cover
While downstream rivers exact their toll
Nature's foreboding warning
Soon ebb and flow diminish
Rain, flood, so omnipotent, has its own life
Sending a message
An innocent drop became a turbulent monster
Return to the waiting, sacred goddesses of the sea

Snow Blanket

Careful, the treacherous, icy snow-covered road
To Tahoe's casinos is a multiple gamble

I tell myself: *Don't be dazzled, frazzled*
The blizzard, bountiful heaps of the big crunchy white
Snowplows in caravans barely keep up
Push mountains of the dirty white stuff to road's shoulder
As we miraculously move towards the casino

Excitement, will I win or lose?
Will I ever get there in this god-forsaken storm?
Where are the state highway crews?
Don't they watch the weather news?
Sure, they scrape piled impediments off the highway
Icy, white, mushy, fresh, blinding

With giant glistening brushstrokes
Paint the crystal, shiny pure antiseptic landscape
Into the forest-laden picture postcard of white,
Heavy snow bend branches jerkily unload
                    the frizzled snow
The icy wind soon subsides in contrast to
The beaming sun's rays, blinding blanket of sparkles

All I want is to get there — gamble, gamble!
While all join in snowball fights, or make their snowmen
Until the cold from ice and snow penetrates the gloves
And puts pink color into the almost frozen ears,
                    lips and face

*Purity starts at birth
and ends there...*

While underneath, the cold grueling brown earth rests
And the ever-present gray rock formations
Topped by a foot or so of the white
Like chiseled, rounded, stone statues
Old rocks withstand these freezing initiations

Let your footprints sink within
The dense whiteness crunches, so pristine
A heavenly fresh momentous experience
Most exhilarating, while your breath circles upward
Until dusk when the cold chilly, icy wind reappears
And all return to the casino, their cabins and their cars

While the white blanket silently stays behind.

Trip to Tahoe in the snow

The world is turning over a new leaf
But a tree has 10,000 leaves
What about all of them?

Illusion from a scenic mountain top

So much imagery – hovering ghosts in space
Seem real, alive, distinct mind provoking
My mind conspires to hear and see this illusion
A transient dream, a wishful apparition
Distorts hammers into our compact senses
Spy the ocean waves – toward the horizon
Peek from high scenic mountaintop
Below, a foreboding, splendid landscape
Its patterns envy glorious natural paintings
View eagle, spreads its wings, soar graceful
And swiftly transcends
Soon, dark foreboding clouds encase my mountain and valley
Landscapes shadows disappear
Among the forest and the rivulets
All an awe inspiring vision!
The quiet before the inevitable
Matches the moan and ecstatic body movement of a lover
Hear the rumble of thunder
The awe of the crash, vibrating lightning
See the gigantic contours of gray dark monster clouds
As I, witness to an actor on the stage,
Transform into new body and character
Top of the world, create a replica of life so real
All our senses are bombarded constantly
Unknown waves pass through our bodies
Continued an instant illusion of time
We don't even shake, rattle and roll!
How quickly life passes by
We wonder: who are we?
How do we fit in?
We are small mobile creatures on two legs,

Foraging we use an odd mixture of concocted shorthand
To communicate and often to miscommunicate
Hurry, down the zigzag mountain trail
Past prickly bushes, flora and fauna
Almost out of breath to civilization
But flash memory scenes repeat of nature's heavenly gift
Only at the cry of the baby's birth
The crash of a car accident
Or parting with a dear friend
Only then does reality dissolve our illusion

The Horizon

From the mountain top - dazzling landscape
Stretch, view beckons
Reach further, touch the horizon I stare! Stare!
Where earth and sky meet
Keep my focus on the fine line between dark and light
Between evil and salvation I step forward, leap, jump
Hoist myself onto a new platform
Rocks, boulders, now circumvent
Carefully I head downward
Thoughts flash
The past vivid, yet much disintegrates
Was it misery, neglect?
Abuse, denigration?
The shock of life's quakes
Like a choking inferno
Careful, as I descend further
Carry my heavy weight with each step
Back to my place, my walls of security
Neglected... outdated... my house of dreams
Oh, I miss the fresh air of those pinnacles
No idea how far my horizon stretches

chapter four: health and aging

Is old?

To my three year old granddaughter
I am a bubble creature
Fearless, friendly, loving.
To my sixteen year old grandson
I am ancient,
Full of idiosyncrasies, mixed
With ridiculous wisdom.
To my yuppie son and daughter
I am not so sharp
An old, tight, slightly selfish man
Hoarder, absent-minded
Flying on his last wings.

But to me
I'm a jolly, dreaming, busy body
A bit forgetful, I am
A cosmopolitan, interested in
The musicals of
Andrew Lloyd Weber,
Mahler at the
San Francisco Symphony
Or Calder's mobiles defying gravity
Football, tennis aces,
Basketball seven-footers

Shapely ladies, scintillation
And conversation are high on my list
Many times of day a surge of
Youth enters my body
Drive to casinos and shoot craps
Sit in the eighth row, center, of many plays
Absorb myself in Beethoven to Shostakovich
Join brisk dancers at senior dance parties
And listen avidly to live jazz or
Dance to the disk jockey's tunes.

I like to be financial advisor,
Investor,
Supervisor of real estate
Sometimes I am clairvoyant,
Though no one listens.
Stay up until 3AM
Sleep
During the day
I plan,
Dream, contemplate
I know the now

Old Folks

Why not be kind to old folks?
Be patient, learn from them
They've shaped you
Built your town
With their sweat and taxes

Ex-warriors, farmers, teachers, policemen
They survived, did not fall between the cracks
Inquisitive, critical, street-smart
Their births and funerals

Each wrinkle exudes experience
Adventures and history beneath their skin
Arthritis, glaucoma, loss of hair
Alzheimer's, shakes, brittle bones
Bent shoulders and slowing movement
But always a twinkle in the eye
A spark of yesteryear

The battery isn't dead yet
There's always room for complaints
But why not show patience?
A hint of kindness, forgiveness
Haven't they earned it?
Are they not your grandparents,
Your older uncles, neighbors?

Who built your libraries, City Hall,
Houses and stores?
They saved land for baseball and soccer fields, schools
Their value system is ingrained in your town
Their love and respect exudes truth
Old in age, yes
Someday, if you are lucky
You'll be one of them!

Every Day

Every day evolves, revolves
With gravity as we experience
Infinite, minute sensations registered upstairs
Our fragile minds perceptive; curious, alive
Some act – most react
Always planning, doing, never satiated

The momentary colossal happenings
The work of innocence
End in an indulgence of more building, moving
Mountains of food and materials
We, too busy, don't even think about it
Until we get hungry and act

We shovel earth into dams
Fill up land with teflon streets and opulent houses
Big canyons of office towers
The whirl of cars, planes, buses humming
To the anvil into a crescendo that we call life

We are those automatons, always busy
So easily, we love and hate
I do not know which one any more
Forgive, but not forget
We are the dreamers, schemers,
Live on our own islands
Pulled into the mainstream of doing

And in old age we melt away ignominiously

We touch many
And many touch us
And sometimes we even say
Thank you

Reminisce; Making the Most of Life

A nonagarian pens rhymes that *pop*
Some are clever, some do *flop*
No more the tranquilizer
Now exercise is the stabilizer

While modern songs blast loud *hip hop*
About guns, gangs and neighborhood
cop
Questioning patriotism to the core
Condemning killings and any war

For me it's Cole Porter, Irving Berlin
Hoagy Carmichael, records turning
Melodious, soothing, sentimental shine
Smooth like familiar, delicious wine

And a timeless kiss
As I reminisce
Picture albums to relive
So much loss, much to grieve

Each precious day, world news entices
Catastrophes, new science ends another crisis
Three healthy meals, a peaceful home
Another happy, lovely day to roam

So I live blissfully on the precipice of time
Express in prose and most creative rhyme
Let my senses taste all that is good
The momentary pleasures of love well understood

Morning Awakening

Awake, I feel, I taste the brilliance of this day
Defy all torment, trepidation that holds sway
I lap and love into the unending fray
An unencumbered volunteer without delay

Too much to do, to worship, to ventilate
So overwhelming too I elevate
From restoration, adoration
With avid ideas, I pass each new station

The broken dish or twisted toy
Disarm, discard and now deploy
Not so easy to replace
A challenging and never-ending chase

And as I mend, just as I break
In innocent and careless wake
Still sparks of end of day twilight
Engaging beautiful and bright

And yet we do what we know best
Reluctant with open mind possessed
For it is Nature's way to pass the greatest day
To keep it all together and avoid disarray

It is foolish, yet we feel this need to please
Our guilt and vanity we often do appease
On the way festivties and food devoured
More assured, less fear, no more the coward

Now busy on the roiling role
Feed my drive, search my soul
Momentum for hope and deed
Mine to harvest and to reap

When everything stops and stays the same
You are probably dead

SHOE SOLDIERS

I awake. In front of my bed are
Two worn black shoes like soldiers
Pointing in opposite directions

White shorts, black socks in juxtaposition
One slipper here, another there
Await my entry into
The unknown day

The ticking clock in rhythm
Says look at me, but
I am too tired
Until it's light again, I will sleep

Shoe soldiers, you must wait
Until I come for you

DREAMER

I, dreamer, seek delicious dessert, free spirit, **lots of it**
Revert to my youth and innocence as if a kid
Replay the first kiss, first fiery love, first tentative sex
Without the daily burden that is far, far more complex

Knock, knock; still seek that inner peace?
Help! Help!
Open your future door with golden keys
Temper some feelings so excessive as I ventilate
To resolve my consternation before it is too late

So as I still search and wonder in my present state
Conjure and dream of yet another wondrous fate
Philosophers and friends do please advise In knowledge
with good luck some sensational surprise

New harbinger of self-sought solace and contentment
Without a ton of things and goods to defy; resentment
God and goddesses of love and life embrace
Ever challenging, now to fill my years of endless space

Flight to Dallas, TX

Reborn

Feel soused, contaminated by an unending binge
My concentrated confused, absent mind now on the fringe
Yawn, yawn heavy eyelids closed
I am a bent and tired like statue half composed
"Snap to it, man", my echo to myself cajole
You are still free, not on parole
Drink coffee, take cold splashing shower
A healthy breakfast will renew brainpower

Sure, I want to forget, to escape
Crawl fetal-like into a sack as a newborn babe
It's a tough, rough dangerous world out there
No cheap ride, just pay the fare.
Can I run away from myself?
Put all my plans and projects on the shelf
Turn on and off creative mind
Impossible solutions solve, find

Rapid dress, coffee, bite and off to work
Seethe as contrarian, avoid in being a jerk
Regain composure, now best that I can do
Perhaps feel happier, and not so blue
This efflorescent stimulated mind
No more a prisoner half blind
Reborn, must do - can do
And to myself be true?

If and when you come to your senses
Don't tell me!

You are the Driver

We are all winners and losers
Who can't read the NYT obituary?
Must have been a short column
What good after you expire?
Morbid? Hell no! Reality!

So live it up now, today
Plan for joy, outdoors, sport, theater
Most joy with happy family
If there is such an animal
Ups, downs, of course
The rollercoaster of your life

Breath the fresh air from the mountaintops
Watch the waves lick the beach
Go touch someone
Hug someone
Even kick someone!

Go give the beggar a buck
Make a positive phone call
Eat a light special meal
Forget yesterday and look forever
Towards tomorrow

One Silver Hair

More silvery hair
No crime; Nature's way to age and care
Touch of wisdom, the sublime
Now I'm mature, more fair

Feel content, a touch of divine
A thousand hairs are yet to follow
Should I despair?
Age gently, keep my disposition mellow

No more the stallion, ace
New balance in the things I do
Easier to watch - than be the leader in the race
Face reality and to myself be true

Must realize, all challenge has its limitation
Still active, plan for betterment, I voted
Some things postpone, others I now ration
Always some change, no status quo and comfort quoted

Feast, love with my dear friends now at leisure
In comfort, settled, more secure
No fear of sudden death or seizure
Despite ailments seek the constant cure

Alert, still active, criticize, I'm a doer
Concerned, experienced, filled with thoughts
Of arts and love a great pursuer
Realize, true inner satisfaction can't be bought

With glee, anticipate most lively, wonderful tomorrow
No apparition, value what I eat, or touch, so real
In harmony, new rainbows drown my sorrow
My goal: to have you join, participate and feel

Make a new life together full of smiles and ease
We tread in unison, embrace love's blessing
I pray forgiveness, want to please
Not perfect, cleanse myself, as I am now confessing

Find time; hold close what I hold dear
Love of my flesh in self-indulgence I cherish
Hold close and kiss the beauty and the goodness here
And may those grand feelings never perish

In time more silver hairs will disappear
And join the aches and pains as I do age
There is the pleasure of new love so dear
Content, I smile, self-satisfied on center stage

I hold your hand in gratitude
As we walk, talk, side by side
Rejoice, value warm friendship with new attitude
Know in my heart I must have done something right!

chapter five: writing

Great Surprise

"Fill me! Fill my pages," cries this book
With witticisms, poems, let it cool!
Stories circle into climactic end
Herald with each reader a new friend

Reports, biographies run their course
Once written down, it's too late for much remorse
Descriptive verbs, the dangling participle
Or baby's teeth tight on the nipple

The passengers take books in curious stride
Headlines of bombs and heroism recalled with pride
Titillating tales in every nook and cranny
Or simply sit, twiddle your thumbs
if there aren't any

Sketches and gossip, such cohesion, esprit de corp
Life is never dull, nor is a murder scene a bore
Last chapter, the stranger queries my demise
Too bad, my rapid recovery to me
and all a great surprise

Poets Paint Life's Dreams

Oh, you poor young soul
Your life not yet whole
Without the joys of poetry to guide
No vision, a blind rider in the night

From where do we generate our expansive dreams
Our hopes, our visions, exultations, our screams?
With ardor, our emotions grow next to new love pangs
Instilled, we visualize word pictures forever in our ranks

Where's the cuddling, the mutual purrs
Our languid bodies wrapped in inviting furs?
Airs of endearment, accolades and gratitude
With drama, comedy and lively interlude?

Where is life's rainbow with beams of magic?
The painted azure sky with pure white clouds do the trick
Typhoon, hurricane, or the scary earthquake's rumble
We're merely bouncing pawns at earth's bidding to tumble

Outside, the devastating storm subsides into a tranquil scene
Still, we remember the agony through which we've been

Mount Shasta, on the way to the
Ashland Shakespeare Festival, OR

Words

Words descend like feathers
Some as heavy lava stones
With dusty, deadly force
Letters pronounced leave a mark
A call for revolution - for change
Plain paper inscribed - the evidence
Words like missiles shoot into the brain
Proclaim - lock horns
Set continents on fire; armies ready

    Folly and insanity
    Level populations
    More words exhort, incite false god believers
    Zealots with religious blindness
    We must endure the lies, false accusations
    Yet with blind venom the masses are intoxicated
    Blinding words! Powerful mesmerizing words!
    When will the insatiable insanity of false saviors stop?
    Avarice, jealousy, ego and hate

Shrouded in the name of preservation
Words eat into the brain
Wise men are thwarted
In a flood of tears and war
Words of peace, offerings melt our hearts
In the concept of our world today
Is peace possible?
Where do words fall
That they are so often ignored?

Only resolve and action will save us

It's the in-between
Between right and wrong
So out of tune
This beating song

Pen

A pen is not a pen
But then again
It's what I write
That's out of sight
Between the index and thumb
Glides calmly, almost numb
Green or red
Almost forget
It giggles, wiggles
Each stroke, each word
Is demonstrated, heard
To deaf ears
Brings ecstatic joy and even tears
A thoughtful wordy link
Until runs dry, is out of ink

WHY?

The word "why," so deadly
So confrontational
So inquisitive
So thorny with sharp edges
Why are you still here?
Why is the why in our vocabulary?
The why am I here?
Why am I not?
The why am I poor?
Why have I been?
So what?
So now?
So how?
So kiss...
But, WHY?
Why, why?

These new poets

These new poets
Spin words like strands of silver
On golden tongues
Glue riveting sentences or chisel them
Into our minds
Raise radiance to heaven
Then drop their victim
And he crashes as an eternal shell into pieces
Preserved and pinned
Like the iridescent
Blue Morpho butterfly

They take flora and fauna
Illuminate Nature's elegance and bestiality
As the bud appears after the winter frost
Blooming into a blaze of color in summer

These new poets uplift
Authorize the art of erotic
With word pictures possess us
They manifest a revolution of norms
They describe the human desire to conquer
Evidenced in severed body parts, a random arm
Head staring blankly
And mass graves

Yet I love the poets' rhythm
Sensitivity, perception
Their wake up call
Prophetic warnings
Vibrant world pictures
With exploding phrases
Stern philosophic soothsayers

They wield the glittering paintbrush
That creates your mirror
Shows you your own imperfections, beauty, savagery

Their language with twists and reflects
You may blast your euphemisms
Hold on tightly to your logic and your senses
While we, the egotistical poets
Are the conscience and irritants within
The bastards of language, full of paranoia
With revealing touch of truth

Dig deep into the hearts and minds
An irritant, a panacea
Like the blossom opens
Or she shark devours
You may not squash or silence us
Many of us have died in fire on the stake
Or been eaten by vermin in dark damp prison cells

Yet I know you will you try to silence us again

Simple

An eclectic critical poet,
Who wrote 3 poems,
Godly, from high up,
Proclaims
That self-published rhymes
Like mine
Are simpleton diatribes
Looked down upon..
Except by me!
I say, I am happy.
My words touch others.
And are absorbed quietly, simply
By all.
And are read by many
Some even call them poems!

When you have a brilliant idea
Write it down!
Test it later
See if it shines
Experiment wisely
And pat yourself on the back!

My stream of writing never ends
Why didn't anyone warn me
it would never stop?

My morning mental writing
Releases hours of frustration within

So many words
So little meaning
And your audience left long ago

Inspiration

The ink changes from black to blood red
Sometimes in the morning I sit up
At the side of my bed
Stark naked, eager to move my pen
Before breakfast
Before I've been fed
Disencumbered in my element
Half awake, I dare to
Let my mind w   a   n   d   e   r
Free flow

Direct
Introspect
Depend and repent
Scribble –

Know most of you are still asleep
Outside the sun peaks gloriously
Over the horizon
Illuminates the bloody dance
Awaits its victim

But that is **tomorrow morning's headline!**

*One of the many classes I gave my
Holocaust talk to in 2016.*

I Am The Poet

I am the poet
> I can shatter the moon
>> Obliterate the sun
> Flatten out earth's curvature
>> Ask annoying personal questions

I am the poet
> Make the maidens swoon
>> Electrify the soldier to the edge of desertion
> Bring the old man's features back to their magnificence
>> Create rhymes; make the child giggle

I am the poet
> Curse arrogance, warn of usurped power
>> Castigate injustice, vilify, demean
> Ask for reprieve, release the incarcerated, the innocent
>> I dig back into the secrets of my childhood

I am the poet
> Fill my chest like Croesus with treasure
>> Want to slay my enemies with venom
> Give comfort to the grieving
>> Implore the heavens to spread truth and purity

I am the poet
> Court the golden-haired, dark-haired
>> Spin disarming rhymes
> Triumph when love turns wild and passionate
>> And melt when cooing lovers entwine

I am the poet
      Protector of the meek and poor
         Alarm, uncover injustice
Spit fire when bribes and dark influence corrupts
         Insidious egotist, critic of society's ills

I am the poet
      My words like leaves wilt
         My prose drowned out by engines
My philosophic warnings go unheard,
         My words unread, though could be influential

I am the poet
      Starved and mocked
         The world of materialism
And modernity will break
         Mock things, yet praise wisdom

I am the poet
      Aspire to pure perfection
         Adore the earth, extol greatness
But rebuke foul inhabitants
         Buttress of truth my shining light

I am the poet
      Demand punishment of the wicked,
         Proclaim justice in an unjust world
Prophesize that good will beget good
         Expose myself for destruction

I am an artist who can tell as ass
from a foot
from a tongue
My heart is in the right place, only slightly to the left

chapter six: ethereal

Dreamers

The voyager, the dreamer
Floats on top like cream
Uplifted by his own fantasy
Unafraid of what comes next

Swims to the next beckoning shore
Determined, inspired, happy
Hedonistic, extrovert
The new, the here, the touch

Let the whole world watch
Our creative, imaginary dreamer
He expects, but doesn't know
What lurks around the corner

Like a blind space ship
Maneuvering among the stars
Comes with him
Takes him

Hang on to your hats, your pocketbook
The blazing road, the beam
Loud joyful yells and cries
Everyone has arrived!

Until all fall off the cliff
Into the expansive horizon

Flying Feather

A snow-white distinct pillow feather, suspended
Floated near my bed; mesmerizing, splendid
Wonder from which bird this precious symbol did shed
Can I fly on this miraculous magical feather instead?

In magic mobile I propel in some delight
The sphere of earth below reflects the moon at night
Clairvoyant, see our world suspended from up high
Mountain ranges, ice poles, oceans catch my eye

A new perspective of global warming first
The deserts dry as plantations lust in thirst
I, way up high, safe, while the globe still spins
Wonder where and which world I'm really in...

Below street lights, human masses, insect-size
Each person unique and special while alive
See them scamper with gadgets in hand
Transform into asphalt jungles precious land

While I gently float above some more
As an observer keeping score
The blinking lights, each a house
Sprinklings of pain and happiness

Until the engine fails... and now
At the cemetery's gate do I arrive
Before I land, peace and tolerance is my plea
Now my flying feather deposits me

Back to reality

You don't have to be perfect
all the time
But it's OK when you are

Share a Dream

Give

    me

       a

           dream

And

    I'll

       fill it

          with treasures

Share them

    proudly

       in

          tomorrow's

             world!

Our reality is

    not things

       but dreams

         feelings

        which touch the heart

Make my spirit

    soar

       into the heavens

         so I can dance

       with the angels

Blithe Spirit

Blithe spirit travels on the sunbeam
On ten thousand dust particles
Transports to a mysterious destination
Open mouth – inhales
Enraptured, captured by the spirit
"Why now – why me?"

He happily acknowledges
Today fate is my bride I shall tarry, romp and ride
The joyous overtones of merriment
Accolades heaved, success granted
Feverish, he decides, almost concurs
Was it all perception, or reality?

Its stamp is tough and lasting
Computer space awarded, the victor
With open arms he/she is received
Believes until the battery dies down
Then the silent shadow vanishes with the sinking sun.

Dream

Spring forward, eyes bulging
    And all the chirping, crackling
        Jumping for joy
            So do I, traipsing, tireless over the
                Dewy wet, green meadow
                    Heading to a farm house

If you asked me "How did I get here?"
    I would frown, rather not wrench it from my mind
        As my body moves down the path
            To a hostel, below rich foliage
                Exhilarated to venture
                    Into the mystery beyond

I ring the bell in my dream
    But the door is unlocked
        "Open up! Open quick!"
            Curious, like a movie clip
                Somewhere out in the country
                  I forgot my suitcase

Full of secrets and consequences

To Relax

To Relax

Completely

I put on brakes

Wipe out all meaning

Let space be my vehicle

Transparent, eyes closed awhile

Now eyes newly open to serenity

Slow breathing

An inner world apart

A smile – in solitude I touch the world

Visions, apparitions, dreams

In space, weightless

The world touches me most gently

Keenly alert

Infinite wonderful

possibilities

Act at Last

Although my eyes lack sharpness
Some hazy shadows, cloudy scenes are observed
In a mature, forgetful but retentive mind
I can still see the eye of the needle distinctly

In a split-second I visualize, conjure
The entire earth seems engulfed by some catastrophe
As each tiny creature in its significant world
Fights for existence

My lifeline catapults, descends
And, like a brown-moth eaten leaf decays
Moves in concentric circles by the hour
I feel a sense of demise

As more leaves turn to mulch
The plots of past dreams tantalize
Yet I revel in shining past moments
Somewhere, somehow I must have done
something right

I stand erect and marvel
Peruse the vast scenery
Gasp at the potential on the horizon
Maybe I'll yet find myself

Let me be me,
and act at last

Invisible Waves

Weird wizardry of thoughts
 Penetrate the most solid walls
  Incubator, spirited
   By invisible incur atmosphere agitated waves
    Sky high, bombarded, digested, piercing
     Bounce, fragment
      To the moon and Mars,
       Smaller than ions or molecules
        Translate into genius thoughts
        Brain like a computer filled with
         An avalanche of ideas
          From it comes the phantom creativity
           It germinates into a working process
            Transfer, reject, accept,
             Enter the framework of the mind
              Rebuild, expose,
               Translate into sound, word,
                Dumfounded exposes
                 Influences all we do
                  Each miracle a touch of our life
                   Even at this moment
                    Thoughts cascade, reason, calculate
                     Into concrete action
                      Ready to change your world today
                       Mine too, as I close my eyes, I'm overcome!
                       Determined, I stand on my own two feet!

He said it so many times that he almost believed it...

Slew a Dragon

Nighttime
We take off one shoe at a time
One sock at a time
Undress
Tired
Lazily
No zest

We slew a dragon today
Had our share of loves and dislikes
Survived confrontation
And for this, we buried the hatchet
Turned over the garden
Schemed against society

It was a full ride
And when I turn
The lights out
I will meet you in my dream world

"Peaceful Dream" painted by Arthur Weil

Soar Like an Eagle

As the eagle soars beside the gray wall cliff
So I, free spirit, soar with wild abandonment, to live
Taste the brisk fresh air next to cheeks and face
Unencumbered, head to an open unknown space

It is that thrill, the joy, adventure and of risk
So full of youth and daring later missed
And as I glide unto the solid footing, full of danger
Soon banter, join the fray now no more a stranger

Adrenalin and fighting spunk my master
At edge precarious I escape disaster
Not yet tamed, must venture to free the unjust
Unselfish risked my body and my life with every thrust

After the wild and experimental years
It's back to family and friends and joy and tears
(But soon demands begs my return to home
Menial routine must stay and cannot roam)

Kowtowed, self discipline my shadow dark
A comprise, defend mine now from the cheats and shark
Value and volunteer community and those in need
In my profession nurture every growing seed

Often mind and early ventures do recall
When goal to change the world meant standing tall
When risk of life and limb meant greatest danger
When all around's so solid and even my enemy is no stranger

chapter seven: people

Away, the Troubles of the Day

Today no leisure
Hurry, hurry, pressure, pressure
All day she's in a roaring rush
Through hail, rain and slush

Help here, help there
She's giving aid everywhere
Answers, errands, doing her duty
Little to show, no reward nor beauty

Self-choice, self-election
Stuck in routine, no satisfaction
Until end of day she makes the trip
Home - no more grind, step and skip

To unlock her cozy apartment door
So pleasant a welcome, as before
Distress, discard, delight, disrobe
No issues, riddles to solve or cope

Fall into bed, happy, vicarious
Free, boundless feelings, vivacious
So liberated, a lovely laugh
Like freedom's boundless path

Enlightened, wonderful to enjoy
Every pillow as soft as a toy
Her smile reaches from ear to ear
Hopeful, eager to see him appear

Waiting for her lover to open her door
A perfect ending, who could ask for more?
So finally, completely washed away
Are all the troubles of the day

If you can only laugh inside
Find an opening and let it all out

Just Happiness

If I were a woman instead of a man
Or a woman who could and still can
Be ambidextrous, bi, or confused
If two spirits in one could be fused
What would critics write to be amused?

But I am ME!
Solid, energetic, entirely free
Maybe rattled, low-rated, sometimes berated
Shaking off showers of advice
All I want is to feel, to love, to be nice

Earn my being, my adequate wage
No wise man nor elderly sage
No muse, no witch, no evil queen
Don't care if it's private or out to be seen

All I want is to follow my avocation
Laugh, have fun, be amused without ration
To ease the world's burden, help the poor
Pray, work and make peace not war

We are all touched by goodness and sometimes hex
We know our sex is most complex
We breathe and we think; we are not blind
Just simple happiness we want to find

And keep.

Rich Recall

A child does not see the end
Yet the aged invalid quite crisp recall
The child wants all now, Right Now!
Because tomorrow is assured, less anticipated
While the old man recounts his fumbling first kiss
His first fight and survival of war
He too was a child once
Yet, upon serious reflection
His spirit smiles as he unravels
His happy childhood

Trust

Platitudes and attitudes
Headlines and oblique flatitudes
Lived a crooked, uneven life
Clever marker, caused much strife

I am thrid from the top, right

Let me, help you, make you rich.
Beneath his mask, "a son of a bitch"

Skilled actor, cheated the rest
Spendthrift scoundrel, did his best
Wasted, swindled, made money disappear
Soon police, FBI, prosecutor appear

Guilty: sentenced to a dozen years
His investors shed no tear
Careful in future of whom you trust
Don't lose your wealth and go bust

The Egotist

The egotist   *b   i   l   l   o   w   s*
spreads his aura, atmosphere
to *conquer/criticize/cajole*

Elevated to a pontific stature
sarcastic, bitter, offensive, coy

Who gives him the right
to enchant us into animals and make us
C   r   a   w   l
in humiliation and shame?

He is a caricature
of who we are

If we listen, an iota of
Truth   *b*
      o
          u
              n
                  c
                      e
                         s   off

Perhaps we will
    Respond
               Act
                    or Applaud

Let us never forget there is
An egotist in all of us.

The Transformation

In my wildest dreams his grotesque stature haunts me
A gruesome caricature of what no one should be;
Disheveled, with stringy dark brown hair
A sunken, pockmarked forehead
Oval shaped head
Cauliflower ears as if he were of wolf's blood
A crooked, beaky, awkward nose
Bushy bear-like brown eyebrows...

Yet underneath this stern and gruesome creature
There used to be a milder man -
Wife and children had long departed
And this reclusive, lonely hermit turned inward,
Brooding in his own awful, primitive abode, a mess.
A miscarriage of justice, an indifferent society
A soul needing rescue, needing help

One day a distant relative savior invaded his home.
Soon an amazing transformation took place;
Curtains thrown open, a cleaning service amply paid,
Soiled furniture and worn appliances replaced.
The radio hummed old melodious tunes,
A new TV screen, computer, telephone invaded the set
Adding ultra-modern tones
Soothing music, fresh aromatic smell
A wholesome atmosphere

Here, an era of healing; of change for the better
A forward-looking, positive attitude
Which overcame all his physical shortcomings
The tortured form now evaporating slowly -
Like a genie from the bottle
Soon a bodily makeover
All, like a fairy tale
A resurrection, ego, manners refined, returned
Budding anew from positive encouragement
Firmly but lovingly urged for the better

Shopping Cart

Thud – thud – thud
The old man, gray-whiskered, stooped
Pushes his rusty shopping basket
His world will never be recouped
Step – step – determined with effort
Slightly bent – tightly gripping the basket rail
In front of him unfurled
His belongings, his livelihood, his world
The soles of his worn shoes touch the
hard cement sidewalk
To the wheels' creaky tune
of creak – creak
Thud – thud – thud
Though bent, disheveled,
Out of the corner of the
Old man's tired, twinkling, sharp, alert eye
He sees all in front
The real world and the unreal
While all about is the hot, humid air
Pressing, almost stifling
As his cart goes – thud – thud – thud

I cannot tell his age – 50 – 60 – 70 or more
His face sun beaten, weary, yet strong
That solid heavy cart in front spells
His castle
His belonging
His blankets
His plastic bags hanging over the sides
A half eaten Mac, a pint of whisky
Could be water or some booze left over from the night before
Some rags, some shaving tools, soap, a towel
Depicting the humanness
Certain pride in a sea of poverty
The remainder of his cart is overflowing with
lots and lots of cans and bottles
Glass and more cans, lids, metal scraps

He pushes on his life and his life estate
          On … on – thud – thud – thud
A sudden stop – habit
          Next to him is the City waste container – a reprieve
          Bending into the container with refuse
          Ah, more cans, more bottles – an accumulative delight
          More rags
Then on to destiny

The basket exudes smells, odors most offensive
A stinky conglomeration of odors
His olfactory glands, long used to this life's aroma
Cans of meat, soup, fish.
It is the small fish can
I can still see the white Cheshire cat
With its long whiskers and sandy eager tongue
Licking the can clean of food.

Each of those cans and bottles
Touched by someone, opened, eaten by someone
Yes, held by a human hand – drunk, eaten
Ready for recycling.

He stoops thud – thud … to the curb
          The spell of heat, the fatigue of the morning
          Woken from a drunken stupor
          He dreams of a cool beer
          The touch of the old lady's strong warm hand
          He feels the chest pain – maybe emphysema
          Too much smoking during the years
          Maybe a touch of kidney trouble
          Or AIDS –

The poison surfaces from time to time
          Next indigestion – not enough solids
          A cramp – another – no one cares but he
            Maybe syphilis or gonorrhea

The old man pushes on.
The world about him oblivious.
Barely a look from passersby

Just a homeless – old beggar
Too many like him –
Aren't they all the same?

The cart starts moving again – thud – thud – thud
A symbol of our time
Thank you Bill Clinton, thank you President Bush
Times are very good –
For some they are good...

The old man now slowly lowers himself
Sits at the curb.
He can still walk.
He is ready for his second drink-a-thon of the day.
And he still lives.
Who cares!
His is joyful – busy world of the moment!

Homeless

The cold, brisk San Francisco evening wind howls
Through the canyon between Davies Hall
and the Opera House
The wind creeps, sneaks
Into the doorways strewn with covered
Hidden, bedecked homeless
Resting in hovels like turtles
In their rhinoceros skin
Peeking out at the guilty, flighty passers-by

Unshaven, covered with ample woolen clothes and blankets
In cardboard houses, each a misfit
Spelling the story of insane bestiality in its most base form
In alcoholic stupor to forget and sleep
Someone shot, beaten,

The mind incoherent, not balanced, confused
The chain of love broken, isolated, suspicious

94

Absorbed with cancer and disease, maggots inside
Admonition, no recognition
Other than that of vermin

Feeling of repeated failure, hopelessness
Numbness of love
Deeply hurt by unforeseen circumstances
The loss of friends matching loneliness

The bottle, the match, the penny, the coke, the crack
The gun, AIDS, syphilis, the needle
Remembrance of cure and salvation
only to succumb to the devil again

The wreck and ravages of human creatures in a sea of wealth
Where is democracy? Where are the churches, the services?
The homeless multiply and suck like leeches for their life
Accompanied by pet dogs, by grocery carts
Always with cups, hats, and open hands begging
Somehow, right here near the Opera House
With its opulence of chandeliers, foyers, high ceilings
Brightly lit, studded with elegant patrons
The voices of the homeless muted, silent, yet in a ring circling
Becoming art of a theater of life
With all living and dead devout
Proud creatures comprising a living cast
The cast of my cousin, my brother, my sister

Someone's mother or father
And I
Who strut and play and say
Let me survive   Let me live
Let me be   Just let me.

The Modern Hermit

Iron door shut
Through bars
One may peek at the sky
Is it the mind or body prisoner
Were it bird or cat prowling
Moving here and there
But he is self-confined
Isolated- shy hermit

Yet in his bosom is a heart
A throb, a feeling
Yet he dare not break out
Too the evil the world outside
Trade one impossible for another
Masked in falsehood and betrayal
Better ignorance, untouched
A soul so whole
So pure, enlightened

Better to be confined than exposed
To the elements of modernity
The latest games, movies, giant sport venues
No here is quiet, simple food
Where the mind can range
Dream and conjure
The body can age slowly with little stress
But who will know when he dies?
Who will remember him
When dust turns to dust?

Nighttime

A great day till sun descended
Bright red-orange hue of dusk and fire
Where eyes and ears were blinkered
Now they are helpless
Targets of the night

Young thugs, the Blood Brothers
Or Coyotes or Hells Bells
All ready to defend their turf
Still just enough light
To walk briskly home

The shadows longer, darker, dangerous
Each gang has their colors: yellow, red, green
Strong, muscular, tattooed
Often fatherless, now show new "family" ties
Only two killings last week

Why in God's name do I
Have to be a prisoner
In my own house?

Time for Retribution

Help me tame my anger, I bleed
I feel the singe, the throb, the need

Rich red blood, a quick attack, accidental knife
Why me? I've been straight as an arrow all my life

The fire storm ignited will, did devour
Such devastating fury and such power

Moral twists, emotions now raw and rude
I want to hit back, revenge, this fearful interlude

Diffuse me; remove these claws of an angry combat cat
An ache, a pain, annoyance at this world gone mad

After hearing from an arbitrary board
Impartial parties weigh the pros and cons, accord

Assess the damage from the conflict, I confess
Still breathe the anger, fire of retribution still possess

Wounded, my love of truth and fairness reprimand
An accident, a folly, a heavenly hand

Injustice, as I witness a liar, perjurer and thief
There's no punishment, all is excused, the hearing: brief

Folly for you who've been wounded, scratched beneath the skin
Time will heal – in meantime bathed in guilt and sin

Wipe out, punish and erase this vicious thought
Revere the prince of peace must hurriedly now come aboard

It's OK to jump on the bandwagon
If you know when to hop off

Civilization

Undiscovered land
Dormant – fertile - waiting
Untilled, virgin, rich, green, muddy yellow-brown
Ripe flower petals droop and beg

When discovered, seeds kernel alive, sprout
The rich rain's magical touch activates
New shades of green, brown, nature's blinding blankets
Bountiful harvest starves in competition with the insects

Suburb and city expansion
Hordes of builders, canyons of skyscrapers
Crops disappear, orchards gone, trees leveled
Money – money – valuable land

Houses, shopping centers, office buildings
Gone the luscious world of animals and nature
The city mushrooms, an asphalt jungle
Someone discovered something

Great music halls, museums, ball fields
Municipal palaces, huge jails, cemeteries
Each retired in his/her cubicle active, waiting
And called it civilization.

Memorabilia for Mars

There will be a day – when
The earth crumbles
And all humanity scrambles away
on huge spaceships with all goods, inventions
Memorabilia for Mars

Omnipotent Power

Omnipotent
Power
So foolish yet so real
    To rise and tower
    So high and lofty
    Soon out of reach

In good faith
We look up to,
Respect, evaluate
    In deference, a touch of awe
    Some mystic aura overpowers us

... Bored Meeting

Confused with the iron dogma
Without latitude, we must study, reason
False Deities and Gods do stifle our breath and creativity
    Choke our spirit, pull rug of all beliefs
    Under a mantle of submission and fear

Only in secret we share our true thoughts
Yet, the powers on high
So out of reach

    Inculcated from childhood
    Traditions, trimmings now imbedded
    Can it not see our misery within?
Our frustration, agony and pain

Blind faith to heal, to tolerate
In disbelief, there's guilt and consequences

Resolve and
Will as we
Cry and struggle to regain
    Our humanity
    Our sanity
A fervent secret wish
"Hope, revel, peace! Our day must come!"

There was a time

There was a time when elections mattered
Old and new immigrants accepted scattered
A bustling, busy country paramount
With happy businesses all abound

There was a time of peace and rest
Where hope and prosperity were blessed
We lived in dignity, respect, routine
Drive-by shootings never seen

There was a time of courtship, sweet
When banana splits were one great treat
Where dare at date you'd steal a kiss
In content family, full of bliss

There was a time where all did work
Be it janitor, teacher, driver, clerk
And human dignity and pride ranked high
No deadly shot disturbed from a drive-by

There was a time of hope and prayer
Where neighbors helped and all did care
In nature's beauty we picked own fruit
Only hunter's gun the prey did shoot

(Not gangs and shoot-outs all around)
There was a time of faith
Of manners, attitudes and grace
Where love and marriage lasted
And honor, friendships not out-casted

If you gamble, and are on a lucky roll, enjoy the ride!
Remember that gravity will take hold eventually;
the devil is waiting for you down there.

Just for Me

Sometimes in my life
All is staged
Some supernatural power
Or the observing Gods
A painful dream, a reality show
Like a cascading mountain boulder, tumbling
I partake, I survive
Just for me

My mind and spirit absorb
Tame my subconscious fears of tomorrow
Overbooked calendar, promises hard to keep
Everywhere the crash, the beat of city noises
Hustle, movement, often blindly automatic
Devour before it devours you
Cars, destinations, self-propelled
Steered dutifully and mechanically
A much blurred vision of life in all directions

The tattered, homeless, bearded man
Standing, hands out, "Can you spare some change?"
The flash of a neckline on a sexy dame
Petite, slender, wiggly, alluring
The feeling soon subsides
Huge advertising signs of unneeded food
A forest of traffic signs just to confuse

And silly, sometimes I even fantasize
This collage, this colossal drama, in juxtaposition
Is like another dusty Western movie
Vivid, visual, bloody, sad
Just for me

The Tyrant Rules

Not the worst tyrant
Nor the last who cleverly has
Befuddled, bewildered his people
Filled the jails, the torture chambers
With his enemies, made many disappear
And robbed his people blind
Police state in our time
Impossible you say - yet here it is!

Inveigled his people for the sake of the revolution
Sacrifice, sheer obedience now
All for a "better tomorrow"
Stole, stashed his country's wealth
In Switzerland and elsewhere
Put an economic noose around his own citizens,
Around the businessmen and entrepreneurs
Collecting national duties, taxes and bribes

He lived in lavish luxury - in secret, of course
His early life fought liberal causes
A chameleon soon became the opportunist
Lies, bribery, false promises still prevail
TV and press extol half-baked accomplishments
Youth idol worships, like a father god
Can do no wrong - all for our good

With his iron fist, lackeys, family members
Opposition was squashed long ago
Concentration-reeducation camps
Control of all the media, phone and TV,
Censors and fear reign everywhere
Newspapers in the hands of a few tycoons
"Stamp out corruption, graft," he extols.

Soon sparks of freedom in secret cells
Dare being caught meant
Torture and execution
You cannot censure the free spirit of expression
Imprison all the minds and thought

More secret cells, clandestine,
All waiting -waiting for the moment
Time is on the side of righteousness
All dictators succumb in the end
Pry open the window of freedom
Of hope and deliverance
Outside there is a storm brewing
And revolutionary cells become image agitated
There is secret encouragement from outside
From free societies who have great emphasis

Birth of a new generation that dares, confronts,
One weekend in spontaneity, mass demonstration
Tens of thousands storm into the main palazzo to protest
At first the polite shot - some are killed
Masses run, regroup and find new leaders
Even army commanders dig humanity
Who dares to shoot into the masses of thousands?

Like during the day of the French Bastille in Paris
Or the Russian revolution in St. Petersburg
The tens of thousands swarm toward headquarters
Guards are overpowered, guns taken from the police
Overwhelmed - The army stands by -
This time now disloyal and angry, tired at its own dictator

The people can once again regain an honest ballot
There is an interim council, cool-headed leaders convened
There are many model systems of constitutions
Referendum, after weeks of debate
The people choose wisely for some kind of justice and equality
Time, too slow, if the most revolutionary instrument is tamed

It will take much, much time before democracy returns
And the rule of law, respect and dignity of man
Is rekindled and better understood.
And new leaders will take the helm, but can we trust them?

The Prisoner!

The prisoner
In fear of life and death
Beaten and starved
Deformed and ill

Shreds of humanity linger, barely visible
Within this agony miraculous hope,
Faith, pain subsides, protective numbness
Another round of torment, torture

Don't let them break you!
Keep your will
Belief – believe in love
Believe in yourself

Not long ago
The same mind exhibited the poet's brilliance
The brain of a scientist, the composer's melodies
The actor, lover on life's stage

Yet now, eyes covered, in dark, damp, hateful cellar
Chained, behind layers of barb-wired fences
Humiliated, degraded, not quite brain washed
In an abysmal, evil, despondent atmosphere

Under the devil's spell
The inquisitor does his dance of death
Obedient warden exhort excruciating pain
The ordained judgment long decided

Soon comes to judgment himself
A larger folly takes over
Vindicates the sanctity of life
Body cremates into gas and dust

Dispersed into the atmosphere from whence it came
Breathed and consumed by all mankind
In today's war of life and self-destruction

Who will be next?

Ever Obedient

The new religion, on airwaves drone
"You are the Children of a new God," in deep sounding tone
On your shoulders a new
Pure civilization will arise that's true
A people healthier and superior
Eliminate all that's inferior
Replace with the new, whose intellect spawns purity
Well-organized, obedient, gives new security

Must protect, ever inspect
Self-chosen, not elect "Believe in us," they proclaim
Enrich this race with wealth and fame
Just follow your new appointed leaders
Alternative: concentration camp feeders
Destroy all impure opposition
Armies on the march upon our decision

Proclaim the source
New inner strength the course
New vision in search of perfection
Our way; the truth is your election
With this new strength and self-assuredness
Mystic angel hovers, she will bless
Open eyes to beauty unsurpassed
To soothing tempo music that will last

Destiny has chosen US to rule
So follow orders, don't act the fool
Well-trained superior equipment
Ignore doomsday rumors and repent
Everywhere we command, have our spies
One thought, one trend make truth from lies
So we must eradicate our insidious opposition
Cripples, demented; must disappear upon my decision

Your Leader stands, admires your selection
He is your choice, your Father for protection
Must swear allegiance, lifelong and forever!
The man is fiendish, mesmerizing, so clever
A propaganda machine as the leaders beckon
Blind obedience must have and reckon
No opposition or dissension tolerated
Free spirit and contrition is not allowed, all kowtowed

The non-believer into re-education camp
As they march to prison on a ramp
New religion to dictate their reason
Cohesive military in this new season
It is our emblem to rule with peace
All open opposition simply must cease.

chapter nine: the future of humanity

We wish most people the best
Dare I tell you what I wish for the others?

Humanity

Humanity
We always evolve, change
The challenge constantly there
Priceless, our very nature so exposed
Yes, I am on trial daily

When we evaluate our lives
Where do we stand now?
Where do we go from here?
Not only in need of food but problems to solve
Challenges

Creative creatures with intellectual
Insatiable appetites
We live in a slumbering dream and
It is time we awaken as the
Heavens will soon rattle our globe
Earth will shake us, scare us
Into a higher and more useful human
Form of existence

We survive, laugh, jovial
We shed tears, mourn, reflect
Yet deep down we return to the marrow
Youth, parents, movies all show us
That iron clad substance is our backbone
So much ahead in the travels of life

Rambling for a better, safer world

So much, so good, so now
So do, so make, know how
What unknown fate did
bring me here?
In fear I act as if my life
is dear

To coin a phrase
Describe a place
Portend of global warning sad
Imbalance of our earth
that's bad

Calamity of chemicals
ignored
In oceans, atmosphere, this
death is stored
Most of us too busy making a living
Most are a generous lot and giving

Much easier to forget
Why worry, guilty fret
OK to sing out of tune
While love and lovers swoon

Learn how to use these new inventions
To tease and stumble now with good intentions
Along the way earn new treasures
Devote to happiness, and health leisure

Conditioned, I share, I do my part
I'll do my job, love it with heavy heart
For now I too want to simply be free
Along the way I'll be a happy me

She yawned at every occasion
and blamed it on the entertainment

Nourish the World

Sacred, sensational springtime re-evaluation
Ripple the earth to shake nitrogen into the soil
Our baby giant is experiencing gigantic growth
The foliage, the buds, new rich green tender leaves

Soon busy bees and butterflies pollinate blooming buds
Magically transformed into rich, ripe fruit
While nearby a carpet of sprawling, ruffled, discarded leaves
Young billowing trees with hues of brown, yellow, green

It is spring, a time of youth, energy and hope, full of bloom
A blanket of colors with many shades and tones
Energized, challenged to be productive
In this uncertain season, soon to reap the harvest

The elements will test, pound, destroy and starve
Oh, say yes, or no - more yes - a season of sink or swim
As immobile plants bear nature's pleasure and brunt
Ever enriching, replenish the thankless earth people

Your expectations rise, at times success is in your grasp
Sidetracked by infatuation, illness, family pressure
Innumerable obstacles and opportunities on this journey
But you will reach a level of accomplishment, and be proud of it

Nature and life intermingle, are ever testing you
The unpredictability and irregularities of spring
Eyes open, keen hindsight, each failure a lesson
Time management and organization - to say no and yes!

Rise early, meet many, beware of the frost, the bugs and bites
See much - but with a cocked eye, cautious
For what is evidenced is often a young man's dream
And visions evaporate in value like the morning dew

With patience nourish yourself and help replenish the earth
And when you grow old, infirm and crooked
Remember, you have done your part
Seeded and harvested
No tree can ask for more as it sheds its leaves

Accept my fate

Breeze into the night
Awake to early morn so bright
Like the waking babe
As a new day takes shape

What's in store?
Who will score?
Ask what for?
Always more

Bedtime without delay
Phased away the day
Felt guiltless in each way
Sleep now, must, without day

Sad that time does soon disappear
Lost, squandered, I now fear
Hold the precious moments in your mind
Survived, found much of life is kind

Too late – no remorse
Change direction, change your course
Renewed effort may succeed
This day's productive still, indeed!

Sorry, day is done, it's too late
Might as well accept my fate
Goofed up, made wrong selection
Steered in
quite the wrong direction

Kind and kinder is a goal
To soothe the soul
And find inner humanity

Life

The spheres of earth and moon
Are forever moving at breakneck speed
This blue and green planet
Carries on its crust all mankind
As earth formations
Yet we creatures, like ants
Go in our crazy, hazy, merry way
We breed, we build brazenly, bombastic
Talk peace, yet forever engaged in wasteful war

We spin our tales in our boxes, as I eternalize
Oblivious of our grand precious earth
Textured, colored, moving patterns
Oceans, lakes in constant flux
Beaches newly born, or washed away
Forests live and die
Species vanish, new mutations are born
Evolution rampant
On the earth's crest, dotted like ant hills
Night lightens with busses, trucks, trains
Quickly a living maze

There is power in silence
But please, not in my coffin

You, me, the infinitesimal
Creature timed from birth
Circling in our own orbit
Reproducing, gravitating
Towards and away from each other
Eking out a livelihood
Existing in our boxes full
Of comfort, food excess clothing
In our cubicles called home
We barely feel the warmth of the sun
Yet live content in its shade
See the brilliance of nature's colors

We think and act like little gods
Yet we are limited on this giant
Cosmos we call earth
Our ancestors long forgotten
As we, the living hurriedly
Venture amused, sexed
Creative, making our tiny marks
Telling our stories, meaningful, real
Alive, lived by billions of us,
And we are just as the satellites and
The stars, forever moving
In silence, lonely, but never eternal

Help a stanger
(help yourself...) smile

Encounters

Each waking hour we encounter
The breeze, light touch, sensation
We observe, we absorb each other
A myriad of ideas, thoughts projected
Bouncing off our well established selves

Let's go to a Masquerade, costumed in vermillion and topaz
Let's follow the switchback trail of mountains past the stumps
Let's walk in the canyons of downtown skyscrapers
Let's decide and project complicated encounters
Let's freeze in thoughtless wonder, listening to our iPhones

As we bedazzle ourselves with computers
Listen and listen more
Texts, inane, primitively respond
Our total being is constantly tested
Weighed, evaluated

We, too busy, forge on, offer blindness
Sometimes we win
An inner urge, a drive, live, do, live
Most often not, as we evaporate into the shadows

Hope for mankind

A frigid mind
A frigid person
Now emerged
From a hot steaming bath
Rubdown
Lotions
The works
A sparkle appears
A grin, a beaming smile
The palpable flesh relaxed
I tell you, there is hope for mankind!

Who We Were, Who We Will Become

The steep staircase of life's learning
Straight, then crooked, curved
Circular, ever upward
On this sensational, scenic trip

It's your life's extravaganza
Influenced, tutored, loved by many
And that heart's desires, tenuous feelings
Impregnated and immersed

Surpass the compact human computer
Stored in the murky mass of messy cells
In our brilliant brain, active, agitated
We envision, recall, digest by experience

Alive in a bloody, maddening world
Gorge heavily on heavenly morsels
Swallow the tortuous acid-laden liquid
Always on the move in a banal, busy world

So sensually sophisticated are we
That we evolve, develop, fathom
Rationalize into complicated patterns
The highest, greatest gift to humanity
Inspire infinite, incredible possibilities

As we dare scratch the heavenly sky
A maturing prototype, we compose, invent
Unlike the finished product from a factory belt
Instead, take action, a rebirth of who we were

Carry our secret banner within our hearts
Aspire to God-like greatness
Almost touch the magnificent magic of the unreachable
Of who we were,
                    who we are, and
                                        who we will become.

Ever know what you never knew,
And when you found out
You wished you hadn't?

From Six Feet Under

A glutton for trophies and punishment
You, so vibrant, violent, alive
I whisper wearily from six feet under
My silent spirit permeates the air
Careful, braggadocio! Gluttony
Must pay the price
Your human wits - labor laborious
Plan, scheme, devise
Your next one thousand, ten thousand feet
Crammed full of goods and gadgets
But for how long?

Move to a larger cloud
The smaller one, until you lie next to
Me for all eternity
In hush, silent spirit
Plan, fastidiously for good results
Soaring success, blazon in your fabulous face
Let vibrant chemical bugs chime
Love songs and idyllic rendezvous
Let smiles and laughter overcome your body
For you are chosen, special
Of all of God's creations, you exceed
Create, devise, adopt
More so than all the lions, tigers
Chimpanzees and Orangutans

My spirit now beneath your skin
Inside your head
For good, clear clarity warm your heart
Away from the war-mongers
The non-believers who preach the gospel
Of power and war
Who relish conflict and lap up the remnants

Of world destruction
Go back into yourself, my spirit urges
Patronize your good feelings
Exude love in all its blazes
Nourish well-earned satisfaction
Shine, love - love lots and be genuine
Partake in the arts of your society
See the world, travel
Soothe the pain - outward and inner
For you are *Human*
You procreate - but you are
Momentary - you are temporary
And as you daily rise

You will fall
But never your spirit determine
You have been chosen in this time
This place to participate in the greatest
Theater of Life

Go - play your parts
And when your time comes
Your spirit will mesh with mine for eternity

LAST RESPECTS

chapter ten: love and other bugs

The Chase

Chased a shapely
Perfumed, slim model
Pursued a crazy exhibition
No more strangers
Now a player
A soothsayer
Yes
No
Why chase?
Just maybe
A lady for all seasons
Whet my appetite
But will she bite?
Right, delight
Without fright
Made a decision
No inhibition
No derision
Just do it
Match
Catch
I did

Just Met

Whispered into her ear
"Miss you already, my dear!"
Don't worry, I am sincere
I am close, I am here

Chemical attraction
Ingrained, self-satisfaction
If she only knew
Of course, I miss her too

Hours ago that we just met
Missed, kissed, one another's pet
Sensations out of the blue
Vibes, infatuation, deep, so true

Another sensual mystery
Called love's chemistry
Fascinated by her darling face
Such beauty, such grace

Tenderly embraced
Pulsation, heart raced
Inner desire, sensation
Magical, such elation

Shortly parted
Just started
"I already miss you!"
You are so dear, so true

Ecstatic, full speed ahead
Euphoric, head spinning, glad
Apart only moments, yet feel so blue
"I miss you, miss you too!"

Is it ordained?
Can this feeling be sustained?
This twosome that we are
Bundled like a shining star

Give Me a Hug

Give me a hug
Surround my bulky body
Warm pressed, comfortable, friendly
I look into your eyes
Only the thickness
Of our clothes keep us apart
Palpitating heart
Exuding warmth
Release – Attraction –
Connected for life
Momentary bliss
Another juicy, pressing kiss
Blind, tormenting, teasing
Blossoming of love
An iota in our moment

We hugged

We hugged - that's all
In our pajamas sometime around 3 or 4 am
We hugged - that's all
Our warm bodies pressed the seconds into hours
Then back to sleep again
It was a deep, strong
Commitment by two loving people
One of them was me
We hugged -
That's all

There was a time when love bugs
Lighted, licked like lollipops, languished
Restrained, controlled, observed
Until the heavy curtain into darkness drawn
Left two lonesome, lovely, searching souls
Chains broken, freed all the passion
Smothered, uninhibited, let loose
And lost in adoration and self-display
As if played most harmoniously in concert
A cachet of duets, for it does take two
Responded with equal vigor, sensitivity
Some call it love, the ethereal thrill
In the heavy heat of moment to moment
Delirious, experimental, such sensual probing
Touch by touch, without strings or convention
Unashamed intimacy, glorious adoration
Lost in that heavenly feeling when nature's
Blood boils over with insatiable desire
Bodies gyrate with blind abandonment
Respond until all is spent in ecstasy
Until the curtain, now slowly restored
Again lets dancing rays of sunbeams dazzle
Leaving a yearning inner feeling, not yet satisfied
So sweet and soft and soothing

Some call it nature's song of love

Missing Parts

love and lose once
pieces   s c r a m b l e d,
reassembled,
with parts   missing

Connections In A Desperate World

Delirious, desperate nonsense with a touch of truth
Brain drain into the atmosphere or outer space
The millions of connections in my cranium, upstairs
Partially short circuit, convoluted and spontaneous
Thinking of fallacies, foolish and fanatic
Like bareback or side saddle? No, no horse for me
Lost in a crappy mountain hotel, abandoned

Damn hot, blossoming bombshell
Searching for electric companionship
Some mystic spiritual connection
Exudes extreme feelings of passion, desire
Blood ritual, tested - floating in space
Insecure, in danger, unsure, eager to escape
As if I was marked by demons

That special, attractive, binding chemistry
Then mine as a recluse to some tiny corner, somewhere
Safer now - celebrate more creative calm
Into a word of meditation, of contemplation

Not immune to the witch's temptations
Away from ideology, war, conflict, stress and danger
Into the self-exile of Nirvana
In search of self-satisfaction, spontaneity
That well-earned peaceful soul of the moment
In some corner of this earth
Even if it means leaving this vault forsaken place

The deeper the love,
the greater the heights
of joy
and pain

I Sing A Song Of Love

I sing a song of love
I sing a song of beauty
Let's tip-toe, dance on the rays of sunshine
Hand in hand, breathe refreshing air on ocean waves
Visit villages and cemeteries, shed happy tears
Sparkle, dance, and reflect in the rich glow of a mirror

I sing a song of values so imbued
Of truthfulness, charity, helping hand
Deep love of nature and its growing mysteries
Of camaraderie, friendship bond
Industrious, perseverance, sharing success

I sing a song of adoration
Your sensual, sculptured facial muscles
Your teasing, tantalizing, curvaceous body
Yet in your sparkling, penetrating eyes
The frame and picture of great beauty, I realize
With a magic wand you touch my heart

I sing a song of love and beauty
To melodies waved into my brain
Taste buds touch tongue in all its intimacy
Colors to befuddle and excite
Extracted out of the magic
Of a rainbow, all the senses burst in
Excitement of closeness
I want to snuggle, cuddle
And caress together in heavenly unity

If you love too hard
You may break your fragile heart

My Valentine

A certain lady stole my heart
Gallant, charming, very smart
She sparkles, kisses most divine
My every day - My Valentine

So we pursue the actors' guild
Our lives of stage and drama, filled
Holding hands, I say you're mine
My every day - My Valentine

So to my Selma, a song I recite
Your stories always my delight
When you're not with me I do pine
My every day - My Valentine

My Valentine, Selma, 2015

My grandest lady of elocution
Patience - else our English full of pollution
A dance with you I'll not decline
My every day - my Valentine

My love bug and my trophy tall
Best time together most of all
My mentor when I drive, miss a sign
My every day - my Valentine

As I hug you in a close embrace
Kiss your lips and welcome face
Invitations to parties we never decline
My every day - my Valentine

As we exercise, travel the world
New vistas, views soon unfurled
Love tennis, music by design
My every day - My Valentine

Tossed salads shared of every kind
Our admiration does our Friendship bind
Most craziness, admit just fine
My every day - My Valentine

On the phone we share our views
Digest, regurgitate the daily news
I beg that you be always mine
My Every day - My Valentine

Shotgun Wedding

The whiz shoots now to lofty heights
He epitomizes major rites
Such as the lover must commit:
Wed her now to avoid an orphaned kid

So concerned some months ago
As her extremities did start to show
She said, "No shotgun wedding, please!"
And he participates in what he sees

So, grandiose, a gorgeous wedding did take place
Their communion now as a friendly phase
But he, still so immature and wild
Could not adjust as father of the child

And in frustration he ran away
Poor girl with baby now must stay
Her family took on the added burden
And both mother, baby simply hurting

She still young; a beauty to behold
While her ex, irresponsible, out in the cold
She, back to school, followed her will
Yet lovingly tends her baby still

The baby soon grew into obedient child
While distant father still confused and wild
Later she remarried, full of happiness
Innocent teenager now in heavenly bliss

So ends the foolish tale of youth
Illicit sex and consequences most uncouth
But like nature's wild animals survive
We humans pair as husband and wife

Most of us attempt to upstand
Paternity suits and problems never end
Most don't want to live our youth again
Between the joys, you'll find tons of pain

Our goal of happiness to be content
In our lifetime may love never end

Love's Passion

It is a wish of flash and fantasy
Translucent, torrid that I see
Your iridescent shape and form
To embrace and break the norm

To hold and feast
Like a ravaged beast
So avaricious
Most delicious

Shower with kisses and with licks
Amorous, no passion that can fix
And as we romp and rave
Gentle, tender, and still behave

And in such magic, blind our action
Intolerable such satisfaction
Experiment, engulfed so deep
Earthy pleasures we want to reap

The seconds into minutes melt
The breath and energy by each is felt
So satisfying, joy abounds
No score, no time to pace, no counts

And so, love blindly soon must part
Each left with feeling in their heart
The memory does linger long
Next meeting know where we belong

Love comes in many packages
and I'll accept them all

Too Late to Cry

No time
Yet all the time
Lists, duties, pressure self-imposed
Meetings, candor, post to post
In a *tizzy dizzy goal-oriented zeal*
Run, jump, move, no time to check how I feel

Sign a contract, match the ware
Goods received, so pay the fare
Quickly kiss the wife, the kids, off to work
Ooze with success, but with sensitivity of a jerk

Bigger house and pool to please
More success so raise the fees
Dinners in and dinners out
Client contracts, that's what it's all about

So the wife then filed for divorce
Neglected kids, now run their own wild course
Suddenly wake up, no wonder why
Love and sensibility long lost, *too late to cry*

You could shower me with praise
and positive words,
but you don't.
Do I have to do everything myself?

chapter eleven: nonsense

Putting Out

Some are putting out
Some are putting in
Some are all about
Some have never been

Since early procreation
Egypt, Greece, early Rome
Each new people
In and out, were on the roam

So your life, my life
Putting out, putting in
It's just the way we live
No histrionics, heroics nor sin

Some are putting out

Some are putting in.

Sometimes it's wiser to exit

than to enter

or not appear

at all

Berkeley Rep theater fund raiser
at the Four Seasons Hotel, San Francisco

Manners

"Manners, manners, dear young man!"
Heard this everywhere, as I ran
I jump ahead, open door
Walk on the curb side and far, far more
At the table hold chair for her, politely ready
Offer subway seat to keep an old gal steady

Despite your manliness and caring
Use less aggression for better faring
You have to have the guts and nerve
She'll give you more than you deserve
She may just toast you like a glowing ember
And give you a night you will always remember

Learned It Long Ago

Hot shot trader
Just escaped the alligator
Boiler platter
Will it matter?
Just don't tell his alma mater
Early sales-call from New York
Sounds pushy, like a dork
Loud voice instructing, "buy this stock"
I say, "No, I'll get stuck"
He persists, "It's a money-maker"
I resist -
Buy a little
Give it a chance
You'll do fine or
Lose your pants
If you really want to know
I lost my pants,
Learned the hard way long ago!

Neither a Borrower Nor a Lender Be

"Neither a borrower nor a lender be
For loan oft loses both itself and friend."
A close relative in dire need
Requested money, and I did feed
After months, she refused to repay
My good deed didn't see the light of day

I am penurious, but not wasteful
From my pocketbook I do money pull
Sadly there was then need for more
I resisted and close the store
Even though we are related
No reason to feel berated

Is it betrayal, or missing the money with which I parted?
Generosity turned sour, should have never started
Of her I'm fond, she needed help so soon
Instead, I could have loaned it to the moon!
Old advice; regardless of being a relative
A shock, a pain when she did stiff

Sternness

It's more exciting
To sit down
Slowly,
Contemplate on
Sights and ideas,
Not to be shocked
Or interrupted
By the
Sternness
Of the
Seat

Obsessively Busy

Are you obsessed?
Not sheltered, blessed
With power
By the hour
Desire for sex
Where's the max?

Intent in praying
Always saying
Besides your honey
Fascinated with money
Learn to closely listen
Always something missin'

Desire to move far, escape
Insular, curse red tape
Too much texting and TV
Hooked, addicted you can see
Always Twitter, Facebook, texts
Latest gizmo - what comes next?

Obsessed, outshine
No privacy the latest sign
Eats my soul unbelieving
No bluff, someone's thieving
Let me be! Sated enough
Immersed, so busy, always rough

As if frozen, statue, stuck
Sheer chase, maybe out of luck

I think the hour has too many seconds

Sometimes

Sometimes
Just sometimes
All the signs, stars
Are aligned
Are in the right position
Short of winning the lottery
Rewards and accolades may come your way

"You are a dear friend"
"Your honesty and demeanor are above reproach!"
"You excel in your work"
"You are one hell of a lover"
Such sweet and expressive language
Is uplifting, embarrassing
But humbly received
For deep down, after all, I earned it!

So
Sometimes...
I wear the right matching clothes
Laud the chef, for he excelled
Give hugs and kisses to my dear one
And this poem I write for her
Extolling all her virtues

Sometimes
Just sometimes
I like myself!
Yes, sometimes
All is right

Right here

Boring Speaker

The speaker mumbles, out of reach
Worst of all, he reads his speech
I'm almost snoring
He's so boring

Without research, vigor nor conviction
Dull recital, uncalled fiction
And me, my mind wanders
Visualizes, imagines, ponders

Our speaker yet drones on and on
Missed the moon and evening sun
Make your point, Sir, so we can wake up
Alas, we suffer, when will you ever stop?

Enough, enough
Of this meaningless stuff!
For he so wise yet stupid to vociferate
Be blocked from entering the pearly gate

The spider on the ceiling
is reeling
I see (you see)
his aim is on me

Lapping Up Your Tale

Too late
No brainteasers please
Just talk,
talk
and talk
Step
by
anticipated
step
Let me   lick   every exciting phrase
Let me travel in your dreams!
Let me know when you find yourself
I'll be here   again
Lapping up your tale

Possessed

It's not the full moon
That makes my system swoon
Nor a delicate, delicious peacock plume
It's her demeanor, it's her perfume
That have occupied my gray cells' room
Addressed, distressed, obsessed
I admit, with her I am possessed

An ass is an ass is an ass
and sometimes it's just our reflection

The Deal

My prospect is to financially succeed
My ego boost; a controlling, dreamer's need
Told you my plan, spilled the beans
But the result's not always what it seems

I shake your hand with great suspicion
Our deal on shaky ground, indecision
Truth bound to my honest marrow, most sincere
Not yet signed on paper, renege I fear

My driven spirit, wealth a must
Now all based on friendship's trust
Investment, meaningful and studied
Chance of success must not be muddied

In life, if you know a healthy path
Measure distance, know your math

For we with our inventions bring fruition
Labored, studied, made with good decision
But some of us in leaps and bounds will crash
Still live on, but without the cash

We are all doubters, unless we become doers
And face reality, then return to being doubters...

My Special Day

With zeal and zest I know this is my day
Aren't four score and ten years enough?
Eagle-eyed, alert and full of contemplation
My day
Not earned, rewarded nor any magical huzzas
Just my day to celebrate
With gratitude, humility, nobleness

You ask "What's so special about today?"
My Ninetieth birthday is at my doorstep
Just me, my own day and all those who care
Too many candles, one is just fine
Too many elaborate, funny, frivolous gifts
At ninety, how much more do I need
To be used only once a year?
Now is the time to shed things
But not you, dear friends

Play my old-fashioned music
Songs of sentimentality and memories
Lift one leg, then the other
Kick the rug or two
Smile at the homemade Crayola cards
Make eye contact with old friends, bond
Maybe a sentimental kiss on the cheek
Grandchildren off in their cyber world

Ninety!
A taste of cake
A grin from ear to ear
Eyes bigger than ever as I
Fake delight over foolish gifts
The doorbell rings; Open, open!
Let the party begin
(It may be my last one!)

My joyous heartbeat, an unexpected gift from nature
So very, very blessed

Fake Facade

I say one thing, but mean another
A contradiction as no other
Though my shadow follows in the sun
I disappear when night has just begun

White lie, in guilt, reverberates
As if I slip and fall on inexperienced skates
For my mind now fabricates illusion
I, most of all, become the victim of confusion

Is it that I want to be loved and to please?
When undressed by truth, brought to my knees
To foolishly scream/dream in a dog-eat-dog world
Upon discovery, accusations are hurled

"You are ungrateful," they accuse and mock
They make me cringe and feel low on luck
To what purpose do I concoct this tall story?
Surely not to please Manfred, Mary or even Morrie

Lost any creative juices to even lie
Ingrained in this illusive life until I die
Meanwhile, I strut like a haughty, guilty liar
So dressed up, elegant in my attire

I wish medicine could cure
the guilty complex
I was born with

You have your ideas
Fate has theirs
And you know who's going to win

chapter twelve: ponderings

Welcome to you, the reader, thank you for sharing some thoughts with me. With this chapter, I spread goodwill, with the hope that you will relish in the love of words and dreams. Turn in the direction of hope, of tolerance. Give thanks to being alive; rejoice! This book, so precious to me, attests to the goal of beauty, of satire, of duplicity and strife. The words echoed are of the benefits of work, of fellowship, and friendship. As you pass through the theater of life, stop, see things as they really are. Shower friends and even foes with goodness and love. With open eyes, ears perked, concentrate on the beauty, marvel at positive expression. Be thankful for family and friends.

Suck the orange slice, readily bite into the rich pear, eyes glazed as you peel bananas. Slowly drink the deep red chardonnay. Love and hug judiciously, joyously! Feel soft, warm skin mesh. Touch all, help all. Beware of setbacks; never flinch in your goals of beauty and truth. Make time and space your master. Like a painter coloring a vast canvas, you too venture into the newness of every day, conscious that time, once gone, never returns. So, dare to involve yourself in three or four precepts, such as charity, truth, education, and fulfillment.

Our vices are hopefully superseded by positive engagement. When did you read last, eat a gourmet meal, make tender, long-lasting, satisfying love? Living is the full utilization of all your faculties. Action is reason; enjoying nourishing food, the collection of music records, starting a project and, yes, following through. Just as you flush the toilet, so flush any hate, wasteful revenge and anger away!

Oh, we are all children. Some wise, some otherwise.

"Some Silly Ifs"

To a writer:
If I stop writing I might as well die; writing is my nourishment

To a soldier:
If I stop fighting, I might as well throw down my rifle, unless the cause is dire and just

To a miner:
If I stop digging I may as well see the light of day

To a prostitute:
If I stop _____ I will be unemployed; easy money no more

To a stripper:
If I stop stripping I will be even more naked

To a dictator:
If I stop dictating, I will be pragmatic politician or live on my wealth

To a lover:
If I stop loving, my heart will break until I find another

To a musician:
If I stop playing, the emotional sounds, dramatic within, my artistry will stifle

To a self-proclaimed ass:
> If I stop being me…
> I've practiced being myself all my life!
> But there are no schools to help me
> So, I admit an ass is an ass
>> But in old age, old asses
>> Albeit self-centered
>> Reap the day
>> And adjust to the magic wonderment
> And content just to end a pleasant evening!

Unshackled

Once in a while a mystic, powerful emotion envelopes us, consumes us, as if in a crazy, irrational, yet happy bubble-sphere. Unbounded, free, we feel fully internally liberated, if only for a passing moment.

Our spirit, thoughts and hopes ascend upwards into the upper atmosphere, all chains broken. Strut free, unencumbered! Let loose; live extemporaneously with joy and no expectations, so blindingly positive it hurts!

It's OK to reach out and touch heaven, to envision the "almost perfect", to parade securely among all mankind as apparitions of a benevolent potentate.

I salute you, world.

My kids; Jeff and Judy, and me

Nature

You, me, we are children of nature; unique and natural, so distinctively different, endowed with natural rights; a life of liberty, equality, fraternity. How we use or abuse this power is another story. We are intellectually powerful, yet puny and often helpless against nature. All emanates from nature; the miracle of birth, the creativeness of being, and even the uncontrollable farewell of death, reverting us to the dust from hence we came.

Next to life, the greatest gift we have is to enjoy nature around us. Never under estimate what our planet has to offer, to respect it, to love and fear it, truly everything around us and beneath us and above us.

As a child I marveled joyously, running freely, catching brown may-bugs, smelling the leaves, the grass, even the dung from the meadow where brown cows were gazing. Many of us tear ourselves away from the daily rat race to co-mingle with nature. We swim in the oceans, ski the lofty mountains, hike, climb or simply meditate and stop the car at some scenic spot. Scared, we watch in awe as the distant tornado nears, or the river floodwaters swiftly cascade off the river banks, eroding all in its path. Fires consume thousands of precious acres, and we hope that droughts don't ruin our crops. All are natural phenomena.Nature, more than anything else, cuts us down to size.

Please take advantage of nature's free gifts! It may be your local park, your flower garden or the next scenic trip you have planned. Smell, feel, hear, see with intent and admiration nature's spectacles, too numerous mention. And when you next itch to get out and move your body, seek out nature to rejuvenate your mind. When you gaze at a waterfall, remember you are part of nature. When you see cows grazing, that is a reminder of our world's natural family. When you kiss the red, bursting cheek of a smiling baby, that's you colliding, interacting with nature in its infancy.

Just as you take care of yourself, so our earth too should be preserved and cared for on a routine basis. Once you fall in love with nature it will be a heady affair, so watch out! My limited space and time leaves it up to you to discover for yourself.

More than anything, nature cuts you down to size.

Drowning in great creativity, from music to stage to fine art

How lucky, at my tender age of 91, to partake twice weekly in the great art forms on offer here in the Bay Area, in San Francisco and Berkeley. I am dazzled by live theater (over forty choices weekly!), great orchestras, operas and super musicals, all enjoyed by lucky me from the center seats. Museums, art exhibits and galleries are also available readily. Oh, what mental feasts abound to enrich and stimulate!

Take time out to admire the display of talent and art forms around you of every kind. Be it baroque music, great oratorios, native music, the world greatest symphonies, ballet, all at your fingertips. The classics; Shakespeare, Broadway productions and famous live speakers all fill my insatiable appetite. There are always second balcony cheap seats available online or last minute offers, even standing room for some shows at little cost. Many people usher and enjoy hundreds of performances for free.

Let us all drown in the arts around us!

Love the Greatest

Love. Those four precious letters can spell out euphoric bliss, deep committed involvement, adoration, lifelong partnership and contentment. And sheer luck if reciprocated! The words "I love you," spoken with deep sincerity, are so special. That phrase is a mystical, magical phenomenon that says "you are my dearest, my closest, my most precious, my partner and best friend". "I love you" expresses a spiritual bond extending and opening yourself to that wonderful creature whom you long for, want to be with, want to share and care for heartily.

Most remarkable are the phases of love with a longtime partner. At first comes the physical attraction, followed by an ever-growing and evolving friendship, the building of the nest, the sharing of tragedies and miseries as well of feast and fun, each partner giving time, support and effort to the other. Through many minor and major crises, love and friendship is tested.

So a wise word to the young person... It's OK to call it love, though it may be simply infatuation, a momentary attraction spirited on by the chemicals in our body. Remember, love is unique, precious, a gift to be treasured, part of the learning curve of life, a lifelong adventure. Love is all-powerful and all-consuming. It is a compromise, unparalleled, instilled to cheer and warm our hearts.

Me, Josh, Judy and Ben

Jeff, Lieutenant Governor Gary Newsome and Jordan, Eagle Scout

Ben, myself and Judy

*My sweetheart Selma
and her son Eric*

Jordan, Jeff and Madison

143

9/17

A Mental Meal of Magical Rhymes and Poems
The Very Best of Arthur Weil, Vol. 1
Weil, Arthur
ISBN: 978-097884568-1

Book Review

Prolific poet Weil (Dare Devilish and Divine, 2011) shares his octegenarian optimism in this liberal helping of inspirational verse.

In 35 themed chapters, interspersing essays and poems with personal photographs, Weil conveys his simple philosophy of mindfulness celebrating life's everyday pleasures. The poems are at their best when approaching nature or reflecting on the author's childhood; *"California Fall"*, for expample, renders autumnal color as a "blanket tabernacle," and *"Before the Storm"* captures "Becalmed icy melt / At sequoia tree trunk." *"Tell Me About Your Past"* chronicles Weil's Holocaust survival and immigration to the United States at age 12. The collection's standout poem, *"Lieselotte",* imagines Anne Frank's thoughts on the train to Auschwitz, punctuated by the haunting refrain "The clatter of the railroad wheels below, ever moving."

144